Extracting Intelligence from RSS News Feeds Using Python and AI

From Global Headlines to Actionable Intelligence

Chet Hosmer

Apress®

Extracting Intelligence from RSS News Feeds Using Python and AI: From Global Headlines to Actionable Intelligence

Chet Hosmer
Longs, SC, USA

ISBN-13 (pbk): 979-8-8688-2772-3   ISBN-13 (electronic): 979-8-8688-2773-0
https://doi.org/10.1007/979-8-8688-2773-0

Managing Director, Apress Media LLC: Welmoed Spahr
Acquisitions Editor: Susan McDermott
Project Manager: Jessica Vakili

Cover designed by eStudioCalamar

Cover image designed by Pixabay

Distributed to the book trade worldwide by Springer Science+Business Media New York, 1 New York Plaza, New York, NY 10004. Phone 1-800-SPRINGER, fax (201) 348-4505, e-mail orders-ny@springer-sbm.com, or visit www.springeronline.com. Apress Media, LLC is a Delaware LLC and the sole member (owner) is Springer Science + Business Media Finance Inc (SSBM Finance Inc). SSBM Finance Inc is a **Delaware** corporation.

For information on translations, please e-mail booktranslations@springernature.com; for reprint, paperback, or audio rights, please e-mail bookpermissions@springernature.com.

Apress titles may be purchased in bulk for academic, corporate, or promotional use. eBook versions and licenses are also available for most titles. For more information, reference our Print and eBook Bulk Sales web page at http://www.apress.com/bulk-sales.

If disposing of this product, please recycle the paper

This book is dedicated to the outstanding team at the College of Applied Science and Technology (CAST) at the University of Arizona. Your support, encouragement, and leadership in cybersecurity education continue to inspire both students and colleagues alike.

I am deeply grateful to Jason, Tracy, Haley, Jake, Carla, Marnie, Angela, and Joey, as well as the entire SOC and FM team. Your dedication to innovation, collaboration, and preparing the next generation of cybersecurity professionals has made a lasting impact.

Thank you for your commitment, your passion, and for fostering an environment where curiosity, learning, and discovery thrive.

Table of Contents

About the Author

Chet Hosmer is the founder of Python Forensics, a non-profit organization that provides research and Python scripts to help with advanced investigative challenges. Chet also serves as a Designated Campus Colleague at the University of Arizona.

Chet has made numerous appearances to discuss emerging cyber threats including NPR, ABC News, Forbes, IEEE, *The New York Times*, *The Washington Post*, Government Computer News, Salon.com, and *Wired* magazine. He has seven published books with Apress and Elsevier that focus on Python Forensics, data hiding, passive network defense strategies, PowerShell, and IoT. In addition, Chet presents at major conferences each year including RSA, TechnoSecurity, HTCIA, Blackhat, and DEFCON.

About the Technical Reviewer

Dr. Gary C. Kessler, CISSP, is president and janitor of Gary Kessler Associates, a training, research, and consulting company specializing in maritime cybersecurity. Gary holds a B.A. in Mathematics, an M.S. in Computer Science, and a Ph.D. in Computing Technology in Education and has been in the information security field since the late 1970s. Co-author of the book *Maritime Cybersecurity*, 2nd edition, and author of dozens of papers on technology-related topics, he is a retired professor of cybersecurity with a research interest in the Automatic Identification System (AIS). An international lecturer, Gary is a guest faculty member at the US Coast Guard Academy, on the advisory board of Cydome, instructor and mentor at the CyberBoat Challenge, a co-founder of the Maritime Hacking Village, and a Fellow in the USCG Auxiliary Cybersecurity Directorate. Gary is also a SCUBA instructor and holds a 50 GT Merchant Mariner Credential. More information can be found at https://urldefense.com/v3/__https://www.garykessler.net__; !!NLFGqXoFfo8MMQ!rXOXyNw7qdngSpZxFvQzMOVp81dJF5CYg2aSzyjrpRB hUvJ595WDAOU2NMzpyRh7YARTgoFfbfNs4Oe6CvE$.

Acknowledgments

My wife Janet, for your unwavering support, encouragement, and belief in me every single day.

Dr. Gary Kessler for his incredible technical editing of this book. I'm deeply indebted for your assistance in making this book better chapter by chapter.

Mike Raggo, for your constant support even in the early days of this project. Your insights into this field and this genre are truly invaluable.

Greg Kipper, for helping shape this book with your thoughtful insights and your visionary view of the future.

Amber Schroader, for always saving me a place to speak at PFIC events. These conferences are consistently on the leading edge of digital forensics and cybersecurity.

OpenAI, for developing large language models that have transformed how we interact with knowledge and making these capabilities broadly accessible.

Guido van Rossum, for creating the Python programming language, which continues to evolve and empower innovation across computer science and beyond.

Julie Lewis, for the opportunity to share the stage with you and the incredible team at Digital Mountain. Your leadership in digital investigations continues to make a significant impact.

Allison Dowd and the Techno Security team, for always welcoming me to speak and for holding a conference that continues to grow and inspire the cybersecurity community.

Kevin DeLong, for your continued support and for creating such a vibrant and welcoming community at the Cyber Social Hub.

This book reflects the remarkable people and communities dedicated to advancing cybersecurity, digital investigation, intelligence analysis, and education. I am grateful to be part of such an inspiring field.

Preface

We live in an age of unprecedented information availability. Every minute, thousands of articles, reports, and observations are published across the Internet, covering topics ranging from cybersecurity threats and geopolitical developments to scientific discoveries and technological innovation. While this abundance of information has tremendous value, it also presents a fundamental challenge: how do we efficiently identify the information that truly matters?

For many professionals working in fields such as cybersecurity, intelligence analysis, research, and journalism, the problem is not the lack of information; it is the overwhelming volume of it. Important insights are often buried within massive streams of news articles, blog posts, and technical reports that are continuously being published across the world.

One of the most reliable and structured ways to access this global information stream is through RSS feeds. For decades, RSS has provided a standardized method for publishing updates from trusted sources. Despite its simplicity and reliability, RSS remains an underutilized tool for large-scale information analysis.

At the same time, advances in artificial intelligence and natural language processing have created entirely new opportunities for analyzing written content. Large language models can interpret text, extracting meaning, identifying entities, evaluating sentiment, and recognizing patterns across vast collections of documents.

This book brings these two powerful capabilities together.

Using Python as the integration platform, we will build a practical system capable of retrieving RSS feeds, extracting article content, normalizing multilingual information, identifying key entities, analyzing sentiment and potential threats, and ultimately applying Agentic AI techniques to determine which information deserves further attention.

Rather than presenting abstract theory, this book focuses on practical implementation. Each chapter introduces real Python scripts that demonstrate how these techniques can be applied to transform raw feed data into meaningful insights. By the end of the book, readers will have a working framework capable of turning large volumes of global information into structured intelligence.

The techniques presented here are especially valuable for professionals involved in open source intelligence (OSINT), cybersecurity monitoring, research, and investigative analysis, but the underlying methods can be applied to virtually any domain where understanding large streams of textual information is important.

The goal of this book is simple: to demonstrate how modern AI tools, when combined with Python and structured information sources, can dramatically improve our ability to discover meaningful insights within the global flow of information.

In short, this book is about moving from raw information feeds to real intelligence.

Foreword

It is both a pleasure and an honor to write the foreword for this book. I have known Chet for more than twenty years, and the work I have seen him do and sometimes had the good fortune to be part of has always been interesting, innovative, and above all, useful. This project is no different.

In this book, you will discover that the next big step in open source intelligence will not come from finding new data; it will come from rediscovering the best sources that are already out there and putting them to work. In this age of generative AI, decentralized communication, and ambient information, Chet shows that RSS feeds remain one of the most underappreciated sources of structured intelligence.

As a career futurist and technologist, I have often spoken about how information would evolve to where it could adapt, learn, and collaborate with people. The methods outlined in these pages represent a tangible step toward that future. By using Python and data-curating techniques, this book illustrates how decades-old RSS feeds can feed quality data into an intelligent ecosystem capable of self-directed analysis and foresight for almost any problem. It also shows that by pairing the clarity of RSS with the interpretive power of artificial intelligence, we can build systems that do more than monitor headlines—they synthesize context, surface anomalies, and anticipate change. In essence, it is a guide to constructing digital sentinels that observe reality in real time.

What makes this book especially valuable is its grounding in trust and structure. In a time when misinformation spreads virally through unverified social media platforms, the need for trustworthy, structured, and verifiable data has never been greater. Through RSS feeds, we gain direct access to curated, fact-checked data that stands up to analytical scrutiny. When combined with large language models and AI agents, these feeds become a dynamic network of global awareness, producing quality insights and actionable intelligence.

For those who actively look for useful innovations, this work is both a toolkit and a guidebook. I'm excited for you and what you are about to learn in these pages.

—Greg Kipper

Introduction

This research grew out of a simple realization: the world is overflowing with RSS feeds (Real-Simple-Syndication) and millions of them, yet only a fraction are actively mined for meaningful insights. Using Python and artificial intelligence, even these overlooked streams of information can be converted into actionable intelligence. And while no authoritative global count exists, web analysis platforms such as BuiltWith[1] have estimated that more than 36 million websites publish RSS feeds.

Why Choose RSS Feeds over Other Sources of Content?

When building an automated intelligence-extraction pipeline, the quality and integrity of the underlying data source are fundamental. RSS feeds offer a unique advantage because they deliver professionally produced, fact-checked, and consistently structured information directly from established publishers. Each feed entry typically includes a well-formed title, author, timestamp, summary, category, and link to the full article. This uniformity dramatically reduces preprocessing overhead and ensures that downstream AI models receive clean, context-rich, and high-signal content that is ideal for summarization, translation, sentiment analysis, and topic classification.

---

[1] RSS usage estimates are based on data provided by BuiltWith, a web technology analysis service (builtwith.com).

In contrast, platforms such as Twitter (X) and Reddit are dominated by short-form, user-generated content that varies widely in grammar, structure, credibility, and intent. Tweets, often emotional, sarcastic, or loose observations, lack the context necessary for reliable interpretation, and most importantly both platforms are heavily polluted by bots, spam, and coordinated mis- and disinformation. Reddit posts can offer deeper discussions, but they remain informal, conversational, and influenced by community dynamics rather than journalistic standards. In both cases, metadata is inconsistent, authors are frequently anonymous, and content often requires extensive cleaning before it becomes usable.

For these reasons, RSS feeds serve as a fertile platform for extracting meaningful and actionable intelligence. Their structured format, editorial reliability, and low noise level make them exceptionally well-suited for automated analysis pipelines, especially when combined with modern tools, algorithms, and techniques. It is important to note that AI intelligent analyses thrive on high-quality input. While social media platforms can still contribute supplemental signals such as early indications of emerging events, RSS feeds remain the most stable, trustworthy, and analytically valuable source for building a robust intelligence-processing workflow.

This overwhelming number of available RSS feeds creates fundamental challenges:

> Identifying high-value RSS feeds aligned with a specific domain or topic

> Programmatically extracting article metadata and content using Python libraries such as feedparser and Newspaper3k

> Handling multi-entry feeds and selecting articles most relevant to your objectives

> Integrating Python with AI models and well-designed prompts to distill the essential insights from curated feed content

Our approach is to bridge the gap between raw RSS data and actionable, AI-driven insight. While millions of websites expose RSS feeds, the challenge lies in identifying the right sources, extracting high-quality content, and transforming that content into meaningful intelligence. Python, combined with modern AI models, provides an ideal platform to accomplish this. The goal is to give you a complete workflow from feed discovery and parsing to advanced analysis and real-world automation so you can build applications that understand, interpret, and react to the world's information streams.

To guide you through this process, the book is organized as follows.

Chapters 1 and 2

Chapters 1 and 2 provide the basis to understand and process RSS feeds. They build the technical foundation by introducing the structure, anatomy, and variations of RSS feeds. You will learn how RSS is encoded, how metadata is represented, and why many real-world feeds do not strictly follow standards. With this background, we introduce practical Python techniques for retrieving and parsing feeds, handling failures and encoding issues, and converting XML into usable Python data structures. By the end of this section, you will have the essential tools needed to reliably ingest RSS feeds at scale.

Chapters 3 and 4

Chapters 3 and 4 focus on preparing and processing feed content. Before meaningful analysis can begin, raw feed data must be normalized, cleaned, and enriched. These chapters focus on preparing RSS content for AI processing. You will learn how to detect and handle missing fields, remove unnecessary formatting, manage multilingual content, and extract full-text articles from linked HTML pages. These chapters show how to build structured representations of feed metadata including author profiles and contextual attributes ensuring that your data is consistent, complete, and ready for analysis.

Chapter 5

Chapter 5 develops methods of extracting actionable intelligence. With high-quality content prepared, this chapter explores how Python and AI can transform RSS feeds into deep insights. You will use Named Entity Recognition (NER) to identify people mentioned in the article, along with organizations, and locations; apply topic modeling and keyword extraction to understand themes and trends; and use sentiment and relevance analysis to evaluate political, social, and global significance. This chapter also covers threat detection and unrest indicators—powerful tools in cybersecurity, governance, and crisis monitoring. The chapter concludes with a complete guide to designing effective AI prompts and building reusable prompt templates for scalable, automated analysis.

Chapter 6

This chapter addresses a key element of Open Source Intelligence (OSINT) by extracting and analyzing sentiment and threats identified within RSS articles.

Chapter 7

This chapter advances from simple AI prompt/response methods such as chatbots to objective-based Agentic AI methods that learn and collaborate from feedback.

Chapter 8

Two unique case studies are presented that demonstrate the power of Agentic AI to extract information from unique RSS feeds that are not cybersecurity related. This demonstrates that our Agentic AI methods can be applied to virtually any domain of interest.

Chapter 9

This chapter examines the future impacts of Agentic AI.

Appendix

The Appendix contains information focusing on

A) Setting Up a Python Environment

B) Third-Party Python Libraries

C) Python Scripts Developed for the Book

D) Key Concepts

Whether you are a developer, analyst, researcher, or simply curious about building automated intelligence systems, this book provides a complete, end-to-end framework for converting global information streams into actionable, data-driven insight. By integrating Python and AI techniques with the enduring power of RSS, you will learn how to build tools that not only gather information but truly understand it.

## CHAPTER 1

Understanding RSS Feed Formats

RSS feeds may appear simple at first glance, but beneath their surface lies a structured and highly flexible format that has evolved over decades of use across millions of websites.

Understanding how RSS is organized, its XML (eXtensible Markup Language) foundation, metadata conventions, and the way content is structured is essential before any meaningful parsing or analysis can take place. By reviewing the anatomy of an RSS feed, it can contain variations and real-world deviations from the standard. The key elements you will encounter in practice include titles, authors, descriptions, links, publication dates, and more. By the end of this chapter, you will have a solid understanding of how RSS feeds are constructed and why that structure matters when building Python applications that rely on clean, consistent data. The good news is that we will be using a third-party Python Library that simplifies the extraction of articles and data elements contained within each article.

Anatomy of an RSS Feed

At its core, an RSS feed is simply an XML document that follows a predictable structure. Every feed begins with a root <rss> element that identifies the version being used, followed by a <channel> block that

© Chet Hosmer 2026
C. Hosmer, *Extracting Intelligence from RSS News Feeds Using Python and AI*,
https://doi.org/10.1007/979-8-8688-2773-0_1

contains the feed's metadata. Inside the channel, you'll find essential details such as the feed's title, publication data, author(s), a link to the website it represents, and a description. These elements help readers and software tools understand the source and purpose of the feed.

The real value of an RSS feed comes from its list of entries. Each item represents a single article, update, or piece of content published by a website or blog page. Items almost always include a title, a link back to the full article, and a summary or description. Many feeds also provide additional fields such as the author, publication date, category tags, and one or more content blocks that may contain an HTML or plain text.

Although the overall layout is straightforward, real-world feeds often include optional elements or custom extensions. Some publishers use namespaces to introduce additional metadata, while others omit fields or use non-standard structures. As a result, understanding the basic anatomy of an RSS feed, what is optional, and what may vary is critical when building tools that need to reliably extract information.

In short, an RSS feed consists of a well-defined structure built on XML with a channel describing the feed as a whole and items representing the individual pieces of content. Once you understand these components and how they appear in different implementations, you can begin to parse and analyze feeds with confidence.

High-Level Structure of an RSS Feed

An RSS feed is simply a text file written in a structured format that computers can easily read. It works like a standardized "news list" that websites publish so that other programs such as apps, readers, or your Python code can automatically check for updates. Each RSS feed contains two main parts:

- **Feed Information**: Basic details about the website, such as its name, a link to the homepage, and a short description.

- **Items (Articles)**: A list of recent posts or updates. Each item usually includes a title, a link to the full article, a short summary, and sometimes the author or publication date.

Although it looks like plain text, the feed follows specific rules using XML tags (such as <title> and <description>) so Python software and support libraries know exactly where each piece of information belongs. This standardized structure—simple, predictable, and widely supported—is what makes RSS so useful for gathering information from many different sources.

RSS feeds follow a formal specification maintained by the RSS Advisory Board. Because the Advisory Board periodically updates and clarifies the standard, readers who want the most accurate and detailed technical information should refer directly to the official documentation.

For detailed information regarding the RSS 2.0 specification at the time of this writing, please refer to the official specification maintained by the RSS Advisory Board.[1]

Simple RSS Example

By providing a simple example of an RSS feed, we can examine each of the major elements one by one and explain their place in the structure of an RSS Feed.

---

[1] *RSS Advisory Board:* `https://www.rssboard.org/rss-specification`

```xml
<?xml version="1.0" encoding="UTF-8"?>
<rss version="2.0">
  <channel>
    <title>Example News Feed</title>
    <link>https://www.example.com</link>

    <description>A simple RSS feed with one article.
    </description>

    <item>
      <title>Sample Article</title>

      <link>https://www.example.com/articles/1</link>

      <description>This is a short article description.
      </description>

      <pubDate>Mon, 10 Feb 2026 12:00:00 GMT
      </pubDate>
    </item>

  </channel>
</rss>
```

Explanation of Each Element of the RSS Example

1. **XML Declaration**

   ```xml
   <?xml version="1.0" encoding="UTF-8"?>
   ```

   This line simply states that the document is an XML file and uses UTF-8 encoding. Every RSS feed begins this way. Note UTF-8 is a way computers store and read text so that **letters, symbols, and emojis from almost any language** can be handled correctly.

2. **The Root <rss> Element**

```
<rss version="2.0">
```

This is the container for the entire RSS feed.
The version="2.0" attribute tells software that follows the RSS 2.0 specification.

3. **The <channel> Block**

```
<channel>
```

Everything inside the <channel> element describes the feed itself—its name, homepage, and basic info.

4. **Feed-Level Metadata**

```
<title>Example News Feed</title>
```

The name of the feed. This is what RSS readers display in their list of subscriptions.

```
<link>https://www.example.com</link>
```

A link to the website represented by the feed.

```
<description>This is a short article description.
</description>
```

A short summary of what the RSS feed is about.

These three fields—**title, link, description**—are the core of the channel metadata and are required by the RSS 2.0 specification.

5. **The <item> Element (An Individual Article)**

```
<item>
  <title>Sample Article
  </title>
```

```
<link>https://www.example.com/articles/1
</link>

<description>This is a short description of the
article.    </description>

<pubDate>Mon, 10 Feb 2026 12:00:00 GMT
</pubDate>

</item>
```

Each <item> represents **one article** or update. Inside it:

<title>: The headline of the article

<link>: A direct link to the full article

<description>: A short summary or excerpt

<pubDate>: The date and time the article was published

RSS feeds often contain dozens or hundreds of <item> elements, but the minimal example above only needs one.

What Makes This Such a Good RSS XML Example?

There are a few reasons why this is a good example of RSS:

- It includes **no extensions**, **no namespaces**, and **no optional fields** that can confuse things as we start to examine more complex RSS Feeds.

- It matches the **RSS 2.0 specification requirements** exactly.

- It is short enough to fit on a single page of the book for easy examination and study.

- It provides a perfect starting point for explaining how Python libraries (like feedparser) read and process feed elements.

## CHAPTER 2

Accessing and Parsing RSS Feeds with Python

Now that we have covered the basics of RSS feeds and the related XML structure, the question becomes how we can retrieve and then parse real RSS feeds from the Internet.

Before we can analyze or extract insights from RSS content, we must first learn how to access feeds reliably and convert their XML structure into usable Python objects. This chapter introduces the practical techniques required to retrieve RSS feeds and prepares you to work with their content programmatically. Throughout this book, we will rely on a widely used third-party Python library called **feedparser**, which offers a simple and consistent way to download, parse, and inspect RSS feeds. The examples in this chapter—and in later chapters—will make extensive use of this library.

Because real-world feeds are far from perfect, we will also address common issues such as encoding inconsistencies, rate limits, unreachable URLs, and feeds that contain malformed or incomplete data. By the end of this chapter, you will be able to fetch, parse, and validate RSS and other Internet or web-based feeds programmatically creating a solid foundation for the processing and analysis techniques introduced in later chapters.

© Chet Hosmer 2026

C. Hosmer, *Extracting Intelligence from RSS News Feeds Using Python and AI*, https://doi.org/10.1007/979-8-8688-2773-0_2

What Is Feedparser and How Do I Install It?

Before we begin working with real RSS feeds, it's helpful to introduce the primary tool we will be using throughout this book: a Python library called **feedparser**. This library takes care of the heavy lifting involved in downloading an RSS or Atom feed and converting its XML structure into clean, easy-to-use Python objects. It is widely used, well-maintained, and ideal for both beginners and experienced developers.

Now, before answering how to install feedparser, I want to be clear about one important point: **this book is not intended to be a complete Python tutorial**. You will certainly learn Python *by doing* as you move through the chapters, but I assume you already have a basic Python environment set up on your computer.

If you are new to Python or if you'd like a refresher there are many excellent resources available. Introductory books, online courses, and free tutorials can guide you through setting up Python, installing packages, and working with essential language features. Any solid beginner's resource will give you the background you need to follow the examples in this book.

Installing Feedparser into Your Python Environment

Installing feedparser is simple. Once your Python environment is set up, you can install the library using the standard Python package manager pip:

From your command line (Windows, Mac, or Linux), type the following command:

```
pip install feedparser
```

After installation, the **feedparser** library can be imported into a Python script using this instruction:

```
import feedparser
```

That's all that's required. As you progress, we'll leverage this library step by step, using real RSS feeds to demonstrate how to fetch, parse, and analyze content in practical, hands-on ways.

Sample Python Script That Uses Feedparser

Here is a simple example on how to use feedparser to extract recent titles from an RSS Feed. The script targets a cybersecurity-related RSS feed from Brian Krebs.

```
'''
feedparser sample script
The script will acquire the last 5 article titles
Appearing in the selected RSS Feed
'''

# Python 3rd Party Libraries
import feedparser    # pip install feedparser

feedURL = "https://krebsonsecurity.com/feed/"
feedName = "KrebsOnSecurity"

titleList = []  # List to Hold acquired titles

feed = feedparser.parse(feedURL)  # Retrieve the contents of
the feed

maxCnt = 5
cnt = 0

if feed:
    for entry in feed.entries:
        cnt += 1
        title = entry.title
        titleList.append([cnt,title])
```

```python
    if maxCnt == cnt:
        break

    print(f"List of Titles from: {feedName}")
    for eachEntry in titleList:
        print(eachEntry)
else:
    print("Invalid Feed or No Feed Response")
```

Step-by-Step Explanation of the Feedparser Sample Script

This simple script demonstrates how to retrieve an RSS feed using the feedparser library and extract the titles of the most recent articles. Let's walk through the code line by line to understand how it works.

1. **Importing the feedparser Library**

   ```python
   import feedparser
   ```

   The script begins by importing the feedparser library, which is responsible for downloading the RSS feed and converting its XML structure into Python objects.

2. **Selecting the RSS Feed to Retrieve RSS Data**

   ```python
   feedURL = "https://krebsonsecurity.com/feed/"
   feedName = "KrebsOnSecurity"
   ```

   Here, you specify the URL and name of the RSS feed you want to work with. In this example, the script targets the **KrebsOnSecurity** feed, a well-known cybersecurity news source. The feedName variable is used later when printing results.

3. **Preparing a List to Store Article Titles**

```
titleList = []
```

This empty list will hold the extracted article titles.
As the script processes each item in the feed, it will
append the title along with an index number.

4. **Downloading and Parsing the Feed**

```
feed = feedparser.parse(feedURL)
```

This is the core of the script. The parse() function
(from the feedparser library) retrieves the RSS feed
from the Internet and converts it into a structured
Python object with attributes such as

- feed.feed—metadata about the feed

- feed.entries—a list of articles (items)

Each entry contains fields such as title, author, published,
and more.
If the feed cannot be retrieved or is malformed, feed will not
contain usable data.

5. **Setting a Maximum Number of Titles to Extract**

```
maxCnt = 5
cnt = 0
```

RSS feeds often contain dozens of articles. For this
demonstration, you only want the five most recent
titles. These variables allow you to count entries and
stop after reaching the limit.

6. **Validating That the Feed Was Retrieved Successfully**

```
if feed:
```

This conditional ensures the feed object is valid before trying to access its entries. It helps avoid errors if the URL is unreachable or returns an unexpected response.

7. **Looping Through Feed Entries**

```
for entry in feed.entries:
    cnt += 1
    title = entry.title
    titleList.append([cnt, title])
```

- feed.entries is a list of article objects.

- Each entry contains fields such as entry.title, entry.link, entry.summary, etc.

- For each article, the script extracts the title and appends it to titleList along with its index number.

8. **Stopping After Five Articles**

```
if maxCnt == cnt:
    break
```

Once the script has collected five titles, it breaks out of the loop. This prevents unnecessary processing of the full feed.

9. **Printing the Results**

```
print(f"List of Titles from: feedName}")
for eachEntry in titleList:
    print(eachEntry)
```

The script prints a header followed by each title in the list. A typical output might look like:

```
List of Titles from: KrebsOnSecurity
[1, 'New Ransomware Variant Discovered']
[2, 'Critical Zero-Day Patch Released']
[3, 'FBI Warns of Credential Stuffing Attacks']
...
```

10. **Handling Invalid Feeds**

```
else:
    print("Invalid Feed or No Feed Response")
```

If the feed was not successfully retrieved, the script notifies the user instead of failing silently.

Why This Script Is a Good Example

- It uses only basic Python constructs (loops, lists, conditionals).

- It demonstrates how to call feedparser.parse(), the most important function in the library.

- It shows real-world considerations, such as validation and limiting output.

- It produces a clean, easy-to-understand result.

This example forms a perfect foundation for the more advanced parsing, extraction, and analysis techniques you'll be introduced to throughout the remaining chapters.

You can easily modify this script in a couple ways. First, you can enter a different URL and feed name. For example, Science Daily provides information related to news with a broad range of science topics of interest. By changing the feedURL and feedName in the script as follows...

```
feedURL = https://www.sciencedaily.com/rss/top/environment.xml
feedName = "Science Daily"
```

...the results would produce the results shown below; give it a try for yourself.

```
List of Titles from: Science Daily
[1, 'Scientists reveal kissing began millions of years before
humans']
[2, 'This engineered fungus cuts emissions and tastes
like meat']
[3, 'Why saving microbes may be the most important conservation
effort ever']
[4, 'Scientists grow a tiny human "blood factory" that
actually works']
[5, 'New report reveals major risks in turning oceans into
carbon sinks']
```

Summary

Now that we've mastered the fundamentals of retrieving RSS feeds with *feedparser* and extracting their titles, we're ready to go deeper. In the next chapter, we will begin processing the full-text content of each feed, transforming raw narratives into structured, meaningful data. We'll also introduce OpenAI into the workflow using it to interpret, classify, and when necessary, translate titles and article text into English to ensure consistent and actionable insights.

CHAPTER 3

Processing RSS Data for AI Analysis

As we move beyond simply retrieving RSS feeds and extracting basic metadata, Chapter 3 introduces the powerful role that OpenAI can play in transforming raw feed content into meaningful intelligence. In this chapter, we will integrate OpenAI directly into our RSS processing pipeline to clean, normalize, and restructure the text produced by diverse global news sources. We will also explore techniques for detecting multilingual titles and article summaries, automatically translating them into English, and preparing all content for deeper analysis in later stages of the system.

By the end of this chapter, you will have a robust, AI-enhanced workflow capable of turning noisy, inconsistent feed data into clean, standardized, and language-agnostic information ready for actionable insight.

The first step in the process is to add the OpenAI Python library to a script and establish a client connection. To do this, you MUST have an OpenAI key.

Obtaining an OpenAI API Key

Before you can integrate OpenAI into your RSS feed processing workflow, you need to obtain an OpenAI Application Programming Interface (API) key. This key uniquely identifies you to the OpenAI platform and allows your Python application to submit requests to the API.

© Chet Hosmer 2026

C. Hosmer, *Extracting Intelligence from RSS News Feeds Using Python and AI*,
https://doi.org/10.1007/979-8-8688-2773-0_3

The process is straightforward:

Note   This following section was provided by OpenAI, and you should visit the OpenAI website for possible updates to the process:

`https://platform.openai.com`.

Create an OpenAI Account

Visit the OpenAI website and sign up for an account if you don't already have one. A valid email address, password, and optional two-factor authentication setup are required.

Navigate to the API Dashboard

After signing in, click on your profile menu and select **"View API keys,"** or navigate directly to the OpenAI API dashboard. This is where all keys for your account are managed.

Generate a New API Key

Click the **"Create new secret key"** button. OpenAI will generate a new, unique API key. Copy this key immediately, this is the only time it will be fully displayed.

Store the Key Securely

API keys must **never** be committed to source code, posted online, or shared publicly. Instead, store the key safely using

- Environment variables (recommended)

- Secure configuration files

- Secrets managers such as those provided by AWS, Azure, or Google Cloud

Add Billing Information (If Required)

Depending on your usage level, OpenAI may require billing information before you can make API requests. Free-tier access may be available, but paid usage unlocks higher rate limits and additional features.

Use the Key in Your Application

Once stored securely, your Python application can load the key at runtime and interact with OpenAI models. Most examples include those in this book assume you've stored your key in an environment variable such as OPENAI_API_KEY.

Integrating the OpenAI Library into Your Python Environment

The next step is to include the OpenAI library in your Python environment. As we did in Chapter 2 when installing the feedparser library, use your command line (Windows, Mac, or Linux) to enter the following command to install the OpenAI library:

```
pip install --upgrade openai
```

Now we are ready to integrate the OpenAI library into our Python script and initialize a client object. This client serves as the interface to all OpenAI model interactions—requests for analysis, translation, classification, and more. The following example demonstrates how to import the library and create a properly authenticated client instance:

```
from openai import OpenAI

client = OpenAI(api_key="YOUR_API_KEY_HERE")
```

New Python Script with OpenAI and Feedparser

In this section, we will build a Python script that combines the strengths of feedparser and OpenAI to perform meaningful, real-world analysis on RSS feed content. The script will walk through a complete workflow—from retrieving multilingual news to translating, enriching, and presenting the results.

This script will perform the following operations:

- **Identify a target RSS feed written in a foreign language.** We will retrieve the feed and prepare it for processing.

- **Extract the first article title and translate it into English.** This demonstrates how OpenAI can assist with multilingual content.

- **Extract the article's author and gather additional information about them.** We'll request brief context or background to enrich the output.

- **Retrieve the full article content and translate it into English.** This turns raw text—regardless of language—into accessible, readable information.

- **Display all collected data in a PrettyTable.** The results will be neatly formatted for viewing, exporting, or integration into future workflows.

Script Part 1

I'm going to break this script up into a several parts—this will allow us to extract key information from the article step by step. The script will process the first (most current) article in the feed. We have chosen to target the RSS feed: `https://www.cisa.gov/cybersecurity-advisories/ics-advisories.xml`. This feed provides information and alerts associated with Industrial Control Systems, security, and vulnerabilities. The feed is provided by CISA (Cybersecurity and Infrastructure Security Agency, a US government agency).

```python
'''
feedparser with OpenAI sample script
The script will acquire an article from a known RSS Feed
and process that article using feedparser to obtain basic
information regarding the first article in the feed
'''
# Python 3rd Party Libraries
import feedparser

feedURL = "https://www.cisa.gov/cybersecurity-advisories/ics-
advisories.xml"
feedName = "ICS Security Feed"

feed = feedparser.parse(feedURL)  # Retrieve the feed

if feed: # Only process valid feeds
    entry = feed.entries[0]  # Use the index method
    title = entry.title      # Obtain the Title
    link = entry.link        # Obtain article Link
    # Get the Author, if available
    author = getattr(entry, "author", "Unknown")
    # Get the Publication Date, if available
    published = getattr(entry, "published", "No date")

    # Print out the results
    print("Results")
    print("=======")
    print("Feed Name:", feedName)
    print("Title:", title)
    print("Link:", link)
    print("Author:", author)
    print("Published:", published)
```

```
else:
    print("No entries found in RSS feed")
```

Script Output

```
=======
Feed Name: ICS Security Feed
Title: SiRcom SMART Alert (SiSA)
Link: https://www.cisa.gov/news-events/ics-advisories/
icsa-25-329-06
Author: CISA
Published: Tue, 25 Nov 25 12:00:00 +0000
```

Next, we will use the same script to obtain results from a foreign language RSS feed: `https://www.heise.de/security/rss/news-atom.xml`, which is a well-known and popular German cybersecurity feed.

Script Output

```
=======
Feed Name: German Cyber Security RSS Feed
Title: Asahi-Brauerei: Daten von fast 2 Millionen Personen
abgeflossen
Link: https://www.heise.de/news/Asahi-Brauerei-Daten-von-
fast-2-Millionen-Personen-abgeflossen-11096297.html
Author: Unknown
Published: 2025-11-28T10:20:00.000Z
```

You may notice that these results indicate no author was provided, and the article link and the title are in German.

Script Part 2

In Part 2 of the script, we will add the ability to acquire the text of the article. Depending on the RSS feed, accessing the article content may be obtained in a couple of different ways.

entry.content[0].value	Full article content (most common)
entry.summary	HTML summary of the article
entry.description	Typical WordPress method
entry.link	Fetch full article from source

To make acquiring the native text and cover all the possible cases, we have created a function that can be included in our scripts. The function is designed to attempt access to the content using each possible method until the content is obtained and return the content to the caller or, if none of the methods are successful, return None.

```python
'''
Function to extract article text
in the native language

The function requires the entry from
the feed to process the text
'''
def extractArticleText(entry):

    # Method 1. Summary/detail (HTML)
    if "summary_detail" in entry:
        return entry.summary_detail.get("value")

    # Method 2. Summary (plain)
    if "summary" in entry:
        return entry.summary
```

```python
    # Method 3. Full content field
    if "content" in entry and entry.content:
        return entry.content[0].value

    # Method 4. Description/detail
    if "description_detail" in entry:
        return entry.description_detail.get("value")

    # Method 5. Description (plain)
    if "description" in entry:
        return entry.description

    # Method 6. If no content in feed… download the
      article page
    if "link" in entry:
        import requests
        try:
            resp = requests.get(entry.link, timeout=10)
            if resp.status_code == 200:
                return resp.text       # native HTML page
        except:
            pass

    return None
```

Now let's add this function into our script and add the text content to our results.

Script Extracting Article Content

```
'''

feedparser with OpenAI sample script – Part II
```

```
The script will acquire an article from a known foreign RSS
Feed and process that article using feedparser augmented
with OpenAI
'''

# Python 3rd Party Libraries
import feedparser        # pip install feedparser

'''

Function to extract article text
in the native language

The function requires the entry from
the feed to process the text
'''

def extractArticleText(entry):

    # Method 1. Summary/detail (HTML)
    if "summary_detail" in entry:
        return entry.summary_detail.get("value")

    # Method 2. Summary (plain)
    if "summary" in entry:
        return entry.summary

    # Method 3. Full content field
    if "content" in entry and entry.content:
        return entry.content[0].value

    # Method 4. Description/detail
    if "description_detail" in entry:
        return entry.description_detail.get("value")

    # Method 5. Description (plain)
    if "description" in entry:
        return entry.description
```

```python
    # Method 6. If no content download the article page
    if "link" in entry:
        import requests
        try:
            resp = requests.get(entry.link, timeout=10)
            if resp.status_code == 200:
                return resp.text        # native HTML page
        except:
            pass

    return None


feedURL = "https://www.heise.de/security/rss/news-atom.xml"
feedName = "German Security Feed"

feed = feedparser.parse(feedURL)  # Retrieve feed Contents

# Only process valid feeds
if feed:

    entry = feed.entries[0]   # Use the index method
    nativeTitle = entry.title
    link = entry.link
    author = getattr(entry, "author", "Unknown")
    published = getattr(entry, "published", "No date")
    nativeText = extractArticleText(entry)

    print("Feed Name:",feedName)
    print("Native Title:", nativeTitle)
    print("Link:", link)
    print("Author:", author)
    print("Published:", published)
    print("Article Native Content:\n", nativeText)
```

Script Output

```
Feed Name: German Security Feed
Title: Asahi-Brauerei: Daten von fast 2 Millionen Personen
abgeflossen
Link: https://www.heise.de/news/Asahi-Brauerei-Daten-von-
fast-2-Millionen-Personen-abgeflossen-11096297.html
Author: Unknown
Published: 2025-11-28T10:20:00.000Z
Article Content:
 Anfang Oktober wurde ein IT-Angriff auf die japanische Asahi-
Brauerei bekannt. Daten von rund 2 Millionen Menschen sind
abgeflossen.
```

As you can see, we have successfully retrieved the Title, Author (which is Unknown), and Publication Date and Time, along with the article content. Because the Title and Content are in German, we would like to have the text readable in English. To accomplish this, we will need assistance from OpenAI.

Adding OpenAI to Our Script

The next step is to translate the Title and Content fields. For this, we will create a reusable function that uses OpenAI to translate the text for us. Before we can tap into OpenAI, we need to add the OpenAI library to our script and create a client object.

```
from openai import OpenAI
client = OpenAI("Your Key Goes Here")
```

You need to insert your key into the call to OpenAI as shown above (and in the Final Script below). Next, we will create a new function that we can use whenever we need to send a prompt to OpenAI for processing.

```python
def OpenAIResponse(prompt, model="gpt-4.1-mini"):
    try:
        resp = client.responses.create(
            model=model,
            input=prompt,
            max_output_tokens=512,
            temperature=0.5
        )
        return resp.output_text.strip()
    except Exception as e:
        # Report any errors
        raise RuntimeError(f"OpenAI failed: {e}")
```

The OpenAIResponse() function is a small, reusable helper that takes a piece of text—called a **prompt**—sends it to OpenAI and returns the AI's answer. Think of it as your own personal "AI messenger." You hand it a question or request, and it delivers that request to the OpenAI model, waits for the response, and then brings the answer back.

Here's what happens step-by-step:

1. **You give the function a prompt**

    You call the function like this:

    ans = OpenAIResponse("When is the next full moon")

    The text you provide is the **prompt**—your instruction or question.

    You can also choose which OpenAI model you want to use, but if you don't specify one, it defaults to

    gpt-4.1-mini

This gives you flexibility without thinking about models every time, but you can specify other models if you like by passing the model of your choice to the function.

2. **The function sends your prompt to the OpenAI API**

Inside the function, a request is made to the OpenAI service using client.responses.create(...).

This is where your message is sent to the AI model.

You can think of it as calling a remote expert and asking them a question.

The function includes a few important settings:

model: Which AI brain to use

input=prompt: The text you want the AI to respond to

max_output_tokens=512: The maximum size of the answer

temperature=0.5: How precise the answer should be

Lower = more predictable

Higher = more creative

These defaults provide a balance of clarity and helpfulness.

3. **The function extracts the AI's reply**

Once the OpenAI API sends back a response, the function grabs the actual text of the answer using

```
resp.output_text.strip()
```

Now we can add this function to our script and use the function to translate the Title and Content of the article in this example.

Final Script

For the final version of the script, I have added the translation of Native Title and Native Content to the results. I have also added a prettytable to make the output more readable. To add the PrettyTable module to your environment, use pip as you have done before by entering the following command at your command line.

`pip install prettytable`

```python
'''
feedparser with OpenAI sample script - Part One
The script will acquire an article from a known foreign RSS
Feed and process that article using feedparser augmented
with OpenAI
'''
# Python 3rd Party Libraries
import feedparser                        # pip install feedparser
from prettytable import PrettyTable

from openai import OpenAI
client = OpenAI(api_key="Your Key Goes Here")

# Reusable OpenAIResponse function
def OpenAIResponse(prompt, model="gpt-4.1-mini"):
    try:
        resp = client.responses.create(
```

```python
            model=model,
            input=prompt,
            max_output_tokens=512,
            temperature=0.5
        )
        return resp.output_text.strip()
    except Exception as e:
        # Report errors
        raise RuntimeError(f"OpenAI failed: {e}")

# Resuable Extract Article Text Function
'''
Function to extract article text
in the native language

The function requires the entry from
the feed to process the text
'''
def extractArticleText(entry):

    # 1. Summary/detail (HTML)
    if "summary_detail" in entry:
        return entry.summary_detail.get("value")

    # 2. Summary (plain)
    if "summary" in entry:
        return entry.summary

    # 3. Full content field
    if "content" in entry and entry.content:
        return entry.content[0].value

    # 4. Description/detail
    if "description_detail" in entry:
        return entry.description_detail.get("value")
```

```python
    # 5. Description (plain)
    if "description" in entry:
        return entry.description

    # 6. If no content download the article page
    if "link" in entry:
        import requests
        try:
            resp = requests.get(entry.link, timeout=10)
            if resp.status_code == 200:
                return resp.text        # native HTML page
        except:
            pass

    return None

#  Feed to process
feedURL = "https://www.heise.de/security/rss/news-atom.xml"
# RSS Feed
feedName = "German Security Feed"

feed = feedparser.parse(feedURL)  # Retrieve the feed

if feed:  # Only process valid feeds

    entry = feed.entries[0]  # Use the index method
    nativeTitle = entry.title
    englishTitle = OpenAIResponse("Translate Title to English: "+nativeTitle)

    link = entry.link
    author = getattr(entry, "author", "Unknown")
    published = getattr(entry, "published", "No date")
    nativeText = extractArticleText(entry)
```

```python
        englishText = OpenAIResponse("Translate text to English:
        "+nativeText)

        print("Feed Name:",feedName)
        print("Native Title:", nativeTitle)
        print("English Title:",englishTitle)
        print("Link:", link)
        print("Author:", author)
        print("Published:", published)
        print("Article Native Content:\n", nativeText)
        print("Article English Content:\n", englishText)

        tbl = PrettyTable(["Category", "Result"])
        tbl.add_row(["Feed Name", feedName])
        tbl.add_row(["Native Title", nativeTitle])
        tbl.add_row(["English Title", englishTitle])
        tbl.add_row(["link", link])
        tbl.add_row(["Author", author])
        tbl.add_row(["Published", published])
        tbl.add_row(["Article Native Content", nativeText])
        tbl.add_row(["Article English Content", englishText])
        tbl.title="RSS Feed Results"
        tbl.align = 'l'
        print("\n\n",tbl.get_string())

else:
    print("No entries found in RSS feed")
```

Final Output Simple Text:

```
Feed Name: German Security Feed
Native Title: Asahi-Brauerei: Daten von fast 2 Millionen
Personen abgeflossen
```

English Title: Asahi Brewery: Data of Almost 2 Million
People Leaked
Link: https://www.heise.de/news/Asahi-Brauerei-Daten-von-
fast-2-Millionen-Personen-abgeflossen-11096297.html
Author: Unknown
Published: 2025-11-28T10:20:00.000Z
Article Native Content:
 Anfang Oktober wurde ein IT-Angriff auf die japanische Asahi-
Brauerei bekannt. Daten von rund 2 Millionen Menschen sind
abgeflossen.
Article English Content:
 At the beginning of October, an IT attack on the Japanese
Asahi Brewery became known. Data of around 2 million people
was leaked.

Final Output: PrettyTable

```
+------------------------------------------------------------------------------------+
|                                 RSS Feed Results                                    |
+------------------+-----------------------------------------------------------------+
| Category         | Result                                                          |
+------------------+-----------------------------------------------------------------+
| Feed Name        | German Security Feed                                             |
| Native Title     | Asahi-Brauerei: Daten von fast 2 Millionen Personen abgeflossen  |
| English Title    | Asahi Brewery: Data of Almost 2 Million People Leaked            |
| Link             | https://www.heise.de/news/Asahi-                                |
|                  | Brauerei-Daten-von-fast-2-Millionen-                            |
|                  | Personen-abgeflossen-11096297.html                              |
| Author           | Unknown                                                         |
| Published        | 2025-11-28T10:20:00.000Z                                        |
| Native Content   | Anfang Oktober wurde ein IT-Angriff auf                         |
|                  | die japanische Asahi-Brauerei bekannt.                          |
|                  | Daten von rund 2 Millionen Menschen sind                       |
|                  | abgeflossen.                                                    |
| English Content  | At the beginning of October, an IT                             |
|                  | attack on the Japanese Asahi Brewery                           |
|                  | became known. Data of around 2 million                         |
|                  | people was leaked.                                             |
+------------------+-----------------------------------------------------------------+
```

Summary

This chapter shows how to move from simply collecting RSS feeds to understanding them with the help of OpenAI. You start by obtaining and securely storing an OpenAI API key, installing the OpenAI Python library, and creating a client object that your scripts can use to talk to OpenAI.

From there, you build a reusable OpenAIResponse() helper function that sends a prompt to an OpenAI model (by default gpt-4.1-mini) and returns the clean text response.

In parallel, you enhance your RSS pipeline with an extractArticleText() function that intelligently pulls article content from multiple possible locations in each feed entry (summary, content, description, or, if necessary, by fetching the page itself).

With these building blocks in place, the chapter walks through a complete, real-world script that combines Python, feedparser, OpenAI, and PrettyTable to process a foreign-language cybersecurity feed.

The script retrieves the latest German security advisory article, extracts the title and article content in their native language, then uses OpenAI to translate both into English.

Finally, it presents all key fields feed name, native and English titles, author, publication date, and both native and translated content—in a neatly formatted table.

You now have a practical, AI-enhanced workflow that turns noisy, multilingual RSS data into clean, standardized, English-readable information ready for deeper analysis and downstream intelligence work.

## CHAPTER 4

Text Extraction and Multilingual Processing

In the previous chapters, we focused on acquiring RSS feeds, parsing their metadata, and preparing a clean foundation for analysis. However, headlines and summaries alone rarely provide enough context for meaningful insight. Real intelligence emerges only when we can reliably extract full article text, understand the content regardless of language, and associate the content with the individual(s) who authored it. This chapter moves decisively beyond surface-level feed data and into the heart of content-centric analysis.

In Chapter 3, we developed a simple reusable function to extract the plain text from an RSS feed. There were several methods provided as not all RSS feeds handle access to the article text in the same manner. The simple method provided here to acquire article text does work; however, if we want to obtain and process the original article, we need to access the article URL (when provided).

Using AI-based language detection, translation, and normalization, we will convert non-English content into a unified, English-language representation while preserving meaning, tone, and contextual nuance. Finally, we will demonstrate how AI can be used to construct lightweight

© Chet Hosmer 2026
C. Hosmer, *Extracting Intelligence from RSS News Feeds Using Python and AI*,
https://doi.org/10.1007/979-8-8688-2773-0_4

author profiles from RSS data—correlating names, publication history, topics, and writing patterns—to add attribution and context to the extracted content. By the end of this chapter, you will have a multilingual-aware, author-enriched text processing pipeline capable of turning raw RSS feeds into structured, intelligence-ready information.

While RSS feeds provide a convenient mechanism for discovering new content, they often include only abbreviated summaries or inconsistently formatted excerpts. Relying solely on this partial data can limit analysis and obscure important context. In this section, we focus on techniques for retrieving full article text from RSS feed entries, including following embedded links, handling HTML content, and removing boilerplate elements such as navigation, advertisements, and inline scripts.

By the end of this section, you will be able to reliably extract clean, readable article text from a wide range of RSS sources, creating a consistent textual foundation for translation, analysis, and enrichment in later stages of the pipeline.

Translating and Normalizing Non-English Content Using AI

RSS feeds are inherently global, and valuable information often originates in languages other than English. Manual translation is neither scalable nor practical for automated analysis pipelines. In this section, we introduce AI-driven techniques for detecting the source language of extracted text, translating it into English, and normalizing the resulting output for consistency across diverse linguistic sources.

The emphasis is not just on translation, but on producing clean, standardized text that preserves meaning, tone, and intent. This ensures that multilingual content can be analyzed, searched, and compared alongside native English sources without introducing bias or distortion.

Let's begin with a simple example that obtains the article text from the associated URL defined in the RSS feed. For this example, we will be using just two third-party Python libraries:

feedparser and newspaper

This initial script demonstrates a simple but effective approach for extracting full article text from an RSS feed entry. While RSS feeds are excellent for discovering content, they often provide only summaries or truncated descriptions. To perform meaningful analysis, we must follow the article link and retrieve the complete source text. This script represents the first step in that process.

Script-Chapter 4-1

```
'''
Extracting and Normalizing RSS Feed Articles Step One
The script will acquire an article from a url link
provided by the RSS Feed
'''

# Python 3rd Party Libraries
import feedparser  # pip install feedparser

# pip install newspaper
from newspaper import Article

# English Language Feed
feedURL = "https://www.sciencedaily.com/rss/top/
environment.xml"
# Retrieve the contents of the feed
feed = feedparser.parse(feedURL)

# Only process valid feeds
if feed:
```

```python
# Obtain the most recent entry
entry = feed.entries[0]

# Obtain the link to the entry
link = entry.link

# Obtain the url of source article
url = entry.link

article = Article(url)
article.download()
article.parse()

fullText = article.text

print(fullText)
```

The script begins by importing two third-party Python libraries. The feedparser library is used to retrieve and parse RSS feed data, converting the XML structure into a Python-friendly object model. The newspaper library is then used to extract the primary article content from a web page, automatically removing common boilerplate elements such as navigation menus, advertisements, and embedded scripts. Together, these libraries allow us to move from feed metadata to full article text with minimal effort.

Next, the script defines the target RSS feed URL. In this example, the feed points to an English-language ScienceDaily environment feed. The feed is retrieved and parsed using feedparser.parse(), which returns an object containing both feed-level metadata and a list of individual entries. A simple validation check ensures that the feed was successfully retrieved before processing continues.

Once the feed has been parsed, the script selects the most recent entry from the feed by accessing the first element in the entries list. From this entry, the article's hyperlink is extracted. This URL serves as the gateway to the full article text, which typically resides outside the RSS feed itself.

The extracted URL is then passed to the Article class provided by the newspaper library. This object is responsible for handling the retrieval and parsing of the article web page. The script explicitly downloads the page content and then invokes the parsing logic, which analyzes the HTML structure and attempts to isolate the main body of the article. This process abstracts away much of the complexity involved in manually scraping web pages.

After parsing is complete, the script accesses the extracted article body via the text attribute of the Article object. The resulting output is a clean, plain-text representation of the article's core content, suitable for downstream processing. Finally, the extracted text is printed to the console, providing immediate visibility into the results.

Although intentionally simple, this script establishes a critical foundation for the remainder of the chapter. It demonstrates how to transition from RSS feed discovery to full-text acquisition, creating the raw material necessary for translation, normalization, and AI-driven enrichment in subsequent sections.

Here is the abbreviated output from the script using the Science Daily RSS Feed:

```
https://www.sciencedaily.com/rss/top/environment.xml
```

```
Researchers examining spiders and scorpions at the Zoological
Collections Laboratory of the Butantan Institute in São Paulo,
Brazil, noticed something unusual on a spider only a few
millimeters long. The animal appeared to be wearing a delicate
pearl necklace. Unsure of what they were seeing, the team
turned to a colleague who specializes in mites for answers.
Ricardo Bassini-Silva, a researcher and curator of the
laboratory's Acarological Collection, quickly recognized that the
bead-like structures were actually mite larvae. Until now, Brazil
had only one documented case of mites that parasitize spiders, and
that species belonged to a completely different family.
```

```
A New Parasitic Mite Identified
Detailed analysis of the spider and its tiny passengers
followed. Using light microscopy, scanning techniques, and
other morphological examinations, the researchers confirmed
they were looking at a new species. The finding represents the
second spider-parasitic mite ever described in Brazil and the
first from its family recorded in the country.
        ..... abbreviated results .....
The discovery also underscores the value of zoological
collections for biodiversity research. The spiders examined
in this study had been stored for years, and the mites went
unnoticed until now. According to Bassini-Silva, collaborations
with field researchers and environmental consulting companies
may soon lead to more samples. He hopes these efforts will
result in the identification and description of additional mite
species associated with a wide range of animals.
```

To illustrate that this approach is not limited to English-language sources, we can modify the script to process an RSS feed published in Russian. This requires changing only a single line in the script the URL that specifies the RSS feed to be retrieved. All other logic remains unchanged, demonstrating that the extraction process itself is language-agnostic.

When the script is executed against the Russian feed, the resulting output is the full article text in its original language. This confirms that our pipeline is capable of acquiring complete content from international sources without any special handling at the extraction stage. At this point, however, the text remains untranslated and unnormalized.

In the sections that follow, we will build on this foundation by introducing AI-driven translation and normalization techniques. These enhancements will allow us to convert the Russian-language output into a consistent English representation and extract key information, enabling meaningful analysis alongside content sourced from English-language feeds.

```
feedURL = "http://feeds.bbci.co.uk/russian/rss.xml"
```

Here is the abbreviated output from the script when accessing the Russian RSS "http://feeds.bbci.co.uk/russian/rss.xml".

«Я не верю в случайность, это было тщательно продумано**».** Украинский военный рассказал, как спасал людей из атакованного поезда
Автор фото, **t.me/dsns_telegram** Подпись к фото, Попавший под удар в Харьковской области поезд
Автор, Би-би-си
2 часа назад
Это перевод материала Украинской службы Би-би-си, оригинал можно найти здесь.
27 января вблизи села Языково в Харьковской области российские войска атаковали беспилотниками **«Герань-2»** пассажирский поезд «Чоп – Харьков – Барвенково».
В результате удара начался пожар, по меньшей мере пять человек погибли.
Позже **«Укрзализныця»** поблагодарила спасателей, врачей, полицию и всех неравнодушных, которые помогали поездной бригаде и пассажирам на месте.

Одним из них был командир взвода ударных дронов **93**-й отдельной механизированной бригады «Холодный Яр» с позывным Омар.
Он рассказал корреспонденту Би-би-си Абдужалилу Абдурасулову о первых мгновениях после атаки, реакции пассажиров и их эвакуации.
«Оператор видел, по кому работает»
«У нас было два автомобиля, которые передали волонтеры, и мы должны были ехать ими на фронт. Но произошла техническая

неисправность, поэтому я решил их оставить на станции техобслуживания и доехать до [города] Барвенково поездом», — рассказал военный.

По его словам, удар первого российского дрона пришелся на другой поезд, который находился на станции в самом Барвенково, и только второй беспилотник попал в поезд, где находился Омар.

«Первый удар достаточно мощный. Опыт подсказал мне, что может быть повторный, поэтому тем, кто был рядом со мной в вагоне, я сказал ложиться. И уже вскоре мы услышали сначала гул, а потом и еще один взрыв. Люди спросили: „Что будем делать?" А я сказал выходить из вагона, потому что если уже было два попадания, значит это массированная атака. И может быть третье», — вспоминает он.

Автор фото, `93ombr.army` Подпись к фото, Командир взвода ударных дронов **93**-й отдельной механизированной бригады Омар `..... abbreviated results .....`

«Когда мы уже добирались с людьми транспортом до Барвенково, еще около **10** дронов летело в сторону поезда. Это был реально массированный обстрел», — уверен военный.

В результате этой атаки, по данным прокуратуры, погибли по меньшей мере пять человек. Один человек считается пропавшим без вести. Идентификация погибших будет возможна после ДНК-экспертизы.

Extracting Linguistic Signals from Native-Language Text

Before translating or enriching foreign-language content, it is often valuable to examine what can be learned from the native text itself. Language carries intrinsic signals that exist independently of author metadata or external attribution. These signals are embedded in word choice, grammatical structure, register, and stylistic consistency, and they can provide important contextual insight when analyzed responsibly. These signals define an author's writing style, often as unique as a signature.

One class of signals relates to linguistic region and dialectal influence. In languages such as Russian, modern journalistic writing is largely standardized, which limits precise regional attribution. However, AI analysis can sometimes identify regional tendencies based on lexical preferences, idiomatic usage, or influence from neighboring languages. These indicators are probabilistic rather than definitive, but they can still be useful when evaluating large volumes of content or identifying outliers within a corpus.

Another strong signal present in native-language text is speaker fluency. AI models can often distinguish between native and non-native writing by identifying unnatural constructions, literal translations, or over-formalized phrasing. This capability is particularly useful in automated analysis pipelines, as it can help flag content that may have been machine-translated, authored by second-language speakers, or generated through coordinated messaging efforts.

Native text can also reveal information about register, formality, and domain familiarity. Vocabulary density, sentence structure, and rhetorical style frequently correlate with professional domains such as journalism, academia, technical writing, or advocacy. These characteristics allow AI systems to infer whether content aligns with institutional reporting, expert commentary, or informal opinion without making claims about the author's identity.

In some cases, AI models may infer generational language tendencies, such as the use of contemporary slang, traditional phrasing, or culturally specific references. These signals should be interpreted cautiously and framed as stylistic tendencies rather than indicators of chronological age. Similarly, while some languages include grammatical gender markers that may leak information in informal writing, gender inference from text alone remains unreliable and ethically sensitive, and any such assessment should be treated as speculative.

Finally, native-language text often reflects cultural and institutional alignment. Writing style, narrative framing, and terminology can reveal whether content follows patterns associated with state media, bureaucratic communication, or independent reporting. These signals are especially valuable when analyzing international content streams, as they provide context that may be diluted or lost during translation.

Taken together, these intrinsic linguistic signals offer a valuable layer of insight that complements—but does not replace—subsequent stages such as translation, sentiment analysis, and author profiling. In the sections that follow, we will translate and normalize this content for broader analysis, while preserving the contextual understanding gained from the native text.

Based on this, we need to utilize AI to analyze the native text prior to any translation. To do so, we need to create a rather complex AI prompt to submit along with the native text to be examined.

Provide a structured analysis of the native text that includes:

- Likely language and writing register (formal, semi-formal, informal)

- Assessment of native vs. non-native fluency, with brief justification

- Any observable regional or dialectal influence, if present, stated as probabilities rather than certainties

- Indicators of professional or institutional writing (e.g., journalistic, academic, technical, bureaucratic)

- Any observable generational language tendencies clearly labeled as stylistic rather than demographic

- Cultural or institutional alignment signals reflected in tone, framing, or terminology

Important constraints:

- Do not assert specific geographic locations, identities, or demographics.

- Treat all inferences as probabilistic.

- If evidence is insufficient, explicitly state that no reliable inference can be made.

Here is the basic prompt that I generated to identify linguistic signals.

You are performing native-language linguistic analysis. Analyze the following text in its original language. Do NOT translate the text. Base all observations solely on linguistic, stylistic, and structural characteristics of the text itself.

We can submit this prompt along with the article text (in the native language) and obtain the resulting analysis. Note, we need to translate the resulting analysis back into English.

```
result = OpenAIResponse(linguisticPrompt)
englishResult = OpenAIResponse("Translate    linguistic
analysis English: "+result)
print(englishResults)
```

OpenAI returned the linguistic analysis in Russian, and we then translated these results for analysis.

Here is the result of the linguistic analysis:

This text is a news report written in Russian and is characterized by the following linguistic, stylistic, and structural features:
1. **Genre and Style - The text is written in the genre of a news article, which is manifested in an objective, informative style of presentation. It uses an official, businesslike style with elements of journalism. The tone is neutral, typical for**

news messages, but there are also reporting elements — quotes and direct statements from participants in the events.
2. **Text Structure** - The text is logically structured, with clear division into paragraphs, each devoted to a separate aspect of the topic. - It begins with a headline that briefly and concisely reflects the main news. - This is followed by a subheading indicating the author and the time of publication, which is typical for news materials. - The main part is divided into informational blocks: statements from key figures, reactions of officials, comments from experts and journalists, descriptions of the current situation. - Introductory words and constructions are used to ensure smooth transitions between parts of the text (for example, "Despite...", "According to...", "Earlier..."). - At the end, there is a conclusion with an overview of current and future events (negotiations, plans).
3. **Vocabulary** - Predominantly neutral, official-business vocabulary: "stated", "agreed", "moratorium", "infrastructure", "press secretary", "negotiations", "shelling", "energy sector". - Includes terms from the fields of politics and international relations, military topics, and energy. - Uses words and expressions indicating the source of information and degree of reliability: "according to him", "according to which", "allegedly", "officially has not yet commented", "unofficial nature of reports". This is typical for journalistic standards of objectivity and factchecking. - Contains quotes with direct speech.

Summary of the Linguistic Processing

The output above demonstrates the value of examining native-language content prior to translation or enrichment. Without relying on author metadata or external context, the analysis identifies the text as professionally structured journalism, characterized by neutral tone, institutional vocabulary, and explicit attribution of sources. These characteristics are consistent with established news-reporting standards and provide immediate insight into the nature and intent of the content.

Equally important is what the analysis does *not* attempt to infer. No definitive regional attribution, demographic profiling, or sentiment classification is asserted. This restraint is intentional and reflects the limitations of text-only analysis when applied to highly standardized professional writing. By treating linguistic signals as probabilistic rather than definitive, the pipeline preserves analytical integrity while still extracting meaningful context.

This step establishes a critical baseline. By understanding how the text functions in its native linguistic and cultural form, subsequent translation and AI-driven enrichment can be performed without losing important contextual cues or introducing unintended bias.

This reinforces pipeline flexibility without complicating the example. *You can obtain the Full Script-Chapter-4-2.py from the GitHub library.*

Building Author Profiles from RSS Feeds Using AI

Beyond the content itself, understanding *who* is producing information can add valuable context to analysis. Many RSS feeds include limited or inconsistent author metadata, making it difficult to assess credibility, expertise, or thematic focus. By learning RSS feed characteristics, we may also be able to infer whether a site is impersonating a credible author or, when faced with incorrect information, making an educated guess about whether the information is merely wrong, repeating misinformation from another site, or generating disinformation. In this section, we demonstrate how AI can be used to enrich author information by correlating names, publication patterns, topics, and writing characteristics across multiple feed entries.

By building lightweight author profiles, you will be able to associate extracted articles with their creators, enabling deeper attribution, trend analysis, and trust assessment within your RSS processing workflow.

We will be using feedparser entries to extract the name of the author(s) associated with this article. In some cases, authors are unknown or not provided within the feed. Here is a simple example on how to obtain and print the name of the author. I chose an article from an ICS (Industrial Control System) Security RSS Feed.

Script Excerpt

```
# Krebs on Security RSS Feed
feedURL = "https://krebsonsecurity.com/feed/"

# Retrieve the contents of the feed
feed = feedparser.parse(feedURL)

# Only process valid feeds
if feed:

    # Obtain the most recent entry
    entry = feed.entries[0]

    title = entry.title
    url   = entry.link
    author = entry.author

    print(author)
```

Script Output

```
Brian Krebs
```

Now that we have the name associated with the Author we can begin to build the profile of Brian Krebs. We will be using OpenAI and prompts to accomplish this. Since we created and

the function `OpenAIResponse` **we can use this to query the large language model for information about the author. We could create separate prompts for this purpose, or instead we could create a single Author Deep Dive Prompt that would be reusable. To accomplish this, we have created a new function:**

```
def BuildAuthorProfilePrompt(author, title, url):
```

The function takes three parameters that we have extracted from the feed, the Author, the Article Title, and the link to the article. All of this will help us ensure that we have the correct author (since there could be more than one Brian Krebs). We want to create a single prompt that is

- Source-anchored (uses the original article URL as ground truth)

- Disambiguation-aware (avoids authors with similar names)

- OSINT-style cautious (no hallucinated emails or affiliations)

- Simple human readable output and results)

Here is the complete code for the new function to accomplish to build an Author Profile Prompt.

You can obtain the Full Script-Chapter-4-3.py from the GitHub library.

```
def BuildAuthorProfilePrompt(author, title, url):

prompt = f"""

Perform author attribution and background enrichment using the
information below:

Author name: "{author}"
Article title: "{title}"
Article URL: "{url}"
```

Use the article URL as the authoritative source for author
identity.

Follow these rules strictly:
1. Treat the article at the provided URL as the ground truth
for author identity.
2. Do NOT merge information from authors with the same or
similar names unless there is strong evidence they are the same
individual.
3. If information cannot be confidently verified, state
"unknown".
4. Prefer primary sources such as publisher bio pages or
verified institutional profiles.
5. Create a list of upto 5 related publication by this author
6. Do NOT invent contact information.

Produce a clear, human-readable author intelligence summary
with the following sections:

Author:
Affiliation:
Background:
Related Publications:
Public Contact Information:
Attribution Confidence:

The output should be concise, professional, and suitable for
inclusion in an investigative report.
"""

```
    return prompt.strip()
```

Now all we have to do is integrate this function into our script.

Here is how we utilize the new function and obtain the detailed author
profile.

```
prompt = BuildAuthorProfilePrompt(author, title, url)
authorDetails = OpenAIResponse(prompt)
print(f"Author Details\n",{authorDetails}))
```

Script Output

Author:
Brian Krebs

Affiliation:
KrebsOnSecurity (independent investigative cybersecurity journalism website)

Background:
Brian Krebs is a well-known investigative journalist specializing in cybersecurity and cybercrime. He is the founder and sole author of KrebsOnSecurity, a widely respected blog that covers topics such as hacking, data breaches, botnets, and cyber threats targeting corporations and government entities. Krebs has a strong reputation for in-depth reporting and breaking major stories in the cybersecurity field. Prior to launching his independent site, he was a reporter for The Washington Post covering cybercrime.

Related Publications:
1. "Spam Nation: The Inside Story of Organized Cybercrime—from Global Epidemic to Your Front Door"
2. "The Target Breach, One Year Later" (KrebsOnSecurity)
3. "Inside the Gameover Zeus Botnet" (KrebsOnSecurity)
4. "How the Mirai Botnet Took Down the Internet" (KrebsOnSecurity)
5. "The Rise of Ransomware and How to Protect Yourself" (KrebsOnSecurity)

Public Contact Information:
unknown

Attribution Confidence:
High - Author identity and affiliation are confirmed by the
authoritative source URL (krebsonsecurity.com) and consistent
with publicly known information about Brian Krebs.

Summary

This chapter marks a decisive shift from metadata-driven RSS processing to full, content-centric intelligence extraction. Moving beyond headlines and summaries, the chapter demonstrates how to reliably retrieve complete article text from RSS feed entries by following source URLs and stripping away boilerplate content. This establishes a clean textual foundation that is essential for meaningful analysis, translation, and enrichment.

Building on this foundation, the chapter introduces AI-driven multilingual processing, emphasizing language detection, translation, and normalization while preserving meaning, tone, and contextual nuance. A key contribution of the chapter is the decision to analyze native-language text *prior* to translation, extracting intrinsic linguistic signals related to register, fluency, institutional style, and cultural alignment. This preserves valuable context that might otherwise be diluted during translation.

Finally, the chapter extends analysis beyond content to attribution by demonstrating how AI can construct lightweight, source-anchored author profiles using RSS metadata, article titles, and authoritative URLs. Together, these techniques transform raw RSS feeds into structured, multilingual, and attribution-aware intelligence suitable for investigative, OSINT, and DFIR (Digital Forensics and Incident Response) workflows.

Operational Benefits

- Enables **full-text intelligence extraction** rather than reliance on truncated RSS summaries

- Provides a **language-agnostic ingestion pipeline**, allowing global content to be analyzed at scale

- Improves analytical reliability by anchoring both linguistic analysis and author attribution to original source material

Analytical Impact

- Preserves **native-language signals** (register, institutional tone, fluency) that are often lost in early translation

- Supports probabilistic, evidence-based inference rather than speculative attribution

- Enhances contextual awareness by correlating content, language characteristics, and authorship

DFIR/OSINT Relevance

- Reduces misattribution risk by preventing author cross-contamination across similarly named individuals

- Enables trust and credibility assessment without relying on external enrichment sources

- Aligns with forensic best practices by favoring restraint, transparency, and explainability

Key Insights Introduced

Translation should not be the first analytical step: Native-language analysis provides unique contextual cues that are otherwise unrecoverable.

Linguistic signals are informative but probabilistic: Responsible analysis requires explicitly acknowledging uncertainty.

Author attribution must be source-anchored: The article URL functions as the ground truth for identity verification.

Human-readable output matters: Analyst-facing summaries improve usability, auditability, and communication.

Innovation and Methodological Contribution

This chapter introduces a **layered intelligence pipeline** that integrates traditional RSS parsing with AI-driven linguistic analysis and cautious author enrichment. The innovation lies not in any single technique, but in how these components are sequenced:

- Full article extraction

- Native-language linguistic analysis

- Translation and normalization

- Author attribution and enrichment

This ordering preserves context, reduces bias, and improves analytical defensibility. By combining automation with disciplined constraints ("unknown rather than guessing"), the chapter presents a scalable yet responsible model for modern RSS intelligence processing—one that bridges the gap between raw data ingestion and actionable insight.

Extracting Actionable Intelligence: Name Entity Recognition

In the previous chapter, we focused on acquiring RSS feeds, translating foreign texts, extracting linguistic signals, and compiling author profiles. In this chapter, we take the next critical step—transforming text into intelligence. News articles, reports, and blog posts are rarely about a single individual; they are dense with references to people, organizations, locations, and institutions that form an interconnected narrative beneath the surface. By applying Python and AI-driven Name Entity Recognition (NER), we move beyond passive reading and begin systematically uncovering *who*, *where*, and *what* matters. This chapter introduces practical techniques for extracting and contextualizing these entities— revealing hidden relationships, emerging actors, and operational relevance laying the foundation for actionable intelligence extraction in the chapters that follow.

© Chet Hosmer 2026

C. Hosmer, *Extracting Intelligence from RSS News Feeds Using Python and AI*,

https://doi.org/10.1007/979-8-8688-2773-0_5

Why Name Entity Recognition Matters: *From Text to Intelligence Signals*

The distinction between *reading content* and *extracting intelligence* is not defined by the text itself, but by the intent of the reader. The same article can inform, document, or reveal—depending on who is consuming it and why.

The Media Reporter: Informing an Audience

For a media reporter, reading is the primary objective. The article is the product. Names, locations, and organizations are included to provide attribution, credibility, and narrative structure, but they are rarely interrogated beyond their immediate relevance to the story. Once the piece is published, its value is largely complete.

The reporter's goal is clarity, balance, and timeliness. Secondary actors may be mentioned briefly and then discarded. Geographic references serve as backdrop rather than signal. Relationships between entities are implied but not systematically examined. From this perspective, the article is *an end state*, not a data source.

The Digital Forensic Investigator: Establishing Facts and Context

For a digital forensic investigator, reading content is a means to corroborate or contextualize evidence. Articles are examined for verifiable facts names, dates, organizations, and locations that can be cross-referenced against logs, artifacts, timelines, and seized data.

- Here, entities matter, but primarily as anchors.

- A name may validate an account holder.

- An organization may confirm infrastructure ownership.

- A location may align with an IP address, device timestamp, or travel record.

However, the investigator typically works within a bounded scope a case, an incident, or a legal question. Once relevance is established or ruled out, attention moves on.

From this viewpoint, content supports the investigation, but it does not *expand* it.

The Intelligence Analyst: Revealing Hidden Structure

For an intelligence analyst, reading content is insufficient. The article is not the product; it is raw material. Every name, organization, and location represents a potential node in a larger network of influences, activity, or intent. The analyst is not asking what happened, but rather

- Who else is involved?

- Who appears repeatedly across sources?

- What organizations intersect unexpectedly?

- Why is this location mentioned at all?

Secondary actors become primary leads. Repetition becomes signal. Omission becomes suspicious. Articles are not consumed in isolation but correlated across time, geography, and source. In this context, Name Entity Recognition is not a convenience; it is a necessity as it enables scale, consistency, and pattern recognition that human reading alone cannot sustain. Thus, intelligence is *extracted*, not read.

Why This Distinction Matters

Understanding these perspectives explains why automated entity extraction fundamentally changes how information is used. When content is treated as narrative, its value is finite. When content is treated as structured data, its value compounds.

This chapter adopts the intelligence analyst's perspective using Python and AI-driven Name Entity Recognition to systematically extract, organize, and contextualize entities transforming individual articles into components of a larger actionable intelligence picture.

Why names, places, and organizations are often more important than verbose content. Common analyst blind spots: secondary actors, implicit affiliations, geographic cues. How NER acts as the **pivot** from raw text to structured intelligence. *Position NER as a mindset shift, not just a technical feature.*

Understanding Entities in Real-World Reporting

The first and most fundamental question in entity extraction is not *how* to extract entities, but *which* entities matter and *why*. Real-world reporting is dense with names, places, and organizations, but not all references carry equal intelligence value. The goal is not exhaustive extraction, but meaningful identification.

People: Beyond the Author

We begin with people's proper names beyond the author of the article. Secondary individuals, quoted sources, officials, executives, witnesses, analysts, or critics often provide the strongest intelligence signals.

These individuals may represent decision-makers, influencers, spokespeople, or emerging actors whose roles are not immediately obvious.

Once a name is identified, the next question becomes whether the individual can be reliably profiled. This is complicated by common names, transliteration differences, and intentional ambiguity. In the previous chapter, we addressed this challenge by anchoring identity analysis to the article title and source URL. That same approach can be reused here with minimal modification, allowing us to associate individuals with context, role, and relevance rather than relying solely on name matching.

Beyond basic identification, we also seek to extract organizational affiliations:

- Functional roles or titles

- Known aliases

- Alternate name spellings

These associations help reduce ambiguity and transform isolated names into traceable entities.

Organizations: Power, Influence, and Alignment

Organizations are often the true drivers behind a narrative. These may include corporations, lobbies or political groups, government bodies, military units, intelligence services, media outlets, non-governmental organizations, or loosely coupled advocacy groups. Identifying organizational entities allows analysts to understand *who benefits, who is implicated*, and *who may be shaping the narrative.* Organizational extraction also enables deeper insight into institutional alignment and interests, patterns of influence across multiple articles, and recurring entities that warrant ongoing monitoring.

In many cases, organizations appear indirectly—referenced through subsidiaries, acronyms, or informal names—making AI-assisted extraction particularly valuable.

Locations: Geography As Signal

Geographic entities, regions, facilities, and countries provide essential context and often serve as indicators of strategic importance. Locations are rarely neutral. They may represent centers of activity, contested spaces, operational hubs, or symbolic targets.

Beyond simply identifying where events occur, we are interested in *how locations are framed.* Are they portrayed as beneficiaries, victims, aggressors, or points of failure? Are certain locations repeatedly associated with specific organizations or individuals? These patterns can reveal emerging hotspots or shifts in operational focus.

From Mentions to Meaning

Taken together, people, organizations, and locations form the backbone of structured intelligence extraction. When analyzed collectively, they reveal relationships, influence, and intent that are rarely apparent through casual reading. This chapter focuses on systematically identifying these entities and capturing just enough context to enable deeper analysis in the chapters that follow.

Important considerations include ambiguity and aliasing, same name, different entities, acronyms and abbreviations, transliteration issues in foreign sources

Why Consistent Extraction Matters More Than Perfect Accuracy

In intelligence-driven analysis, the objective is not perfection, it is **repeatability and signal detection at scale**. While perfect entity identification may sound like the ideal goal, it is rarely achievable in real-world reporting and, more importantly, it is not required to produce meaningful intelligence. Indeed, seeking perfection often causes the investigator to experience "paralysis by analysis." Investigators and Intelligences analyst should not be hasty in connecting the dots, you also need to be able to understand emerging patterns without having to see every single point of data.

The Reality of Imperfect Data

News articles are written for human readers, not analytical systems. Names may be abbreviated, misspelled, transliterated differently across languages, or intentionally vague. Organizations may be referenced indirectly or through acronyms. Locations may be implied rather than explicitly stated. Expecting flawless extraction from such input is unrealistic and, in many cases, unnecessary.

Instead, intelligence value emerges when extraction methods behave **consistently** across large volumes of content.

Leveraging AI-Assisted NER with Python by Crafting Prompts for Entity Extraction

When using AI-assisted **Name Entity Recognition**, prompt design becomes the controlling factor in extraction quality. The objective is not creativity, but discipline. Prompts must be structured to minimize hallucination, accurately identify relevant entities such as people, organizations, and locations and present results in a clear, analyst-friendly format.

What are hallucinations? Hallucinations in the context of Large Language Models refer to outputs that are syntactically coherent and confidently presented, but factually incorrect, unsupported by the source material, or entirely fabricated. These errors occur when the model generates information that was not explicitly grounded in the provided input or verifiable data. In order to avoid hallucinations, or other errors, we must create prompts that guard against this.

Effective prompts emphasize precision over verbosity and consistency over cleverness. Results should be concise, factual, and easy to scan, allowing analysts to focus on the intelligence value of the extracted entities rather than the language used to describe them. In this context, "just the facts" is not a limitation but a design goal.

Implementing Entity Extraction in Python

Now that we understand what entities we are looking for and why, our next step is to operationalize the process in Python. The goal of this section is to demonstrate a practical workflow that takes normalized article text as input and returns a structured list of people, organizations, and locations as output. We will begin with a simple extraction prompt to establish a baseline, then evolve it into more controlled and analyst-friendly prompts that reduce hallucination, improve consistency, and produce results that are easy to parse, store, and compare across articles.

To keep the workflow reliable, we will separate **entity identification** from **entity profiling**. First, we extract candidate entities with supporting context from the article itself. Then, only when needed, we run a second step that attempts deeper profiling and clearly labels uncertainty when name collisions or ambiguous references exist.

Example: NER Identification (Extraction-First)

Effective prompt development is both art and engineering. Large Language Models respond not just to what we ask, but to how we constrain and structure the request. Clear objectives, explicit boundaries, and defined output formats are essential. Prompts must be developed, tested, evaluated, refined, and tested again. Iteration is not optional it is the mechanism through which reliability and analytical discipline are achieved.

Here is our current NERExtractionPrompt. Note like most complex prompts, this is still a work in progress; however, it provides excellent results as is.

```
NERExtractionPrompt = f"""
Examine the following article text and extract named entities.

Identify:
- People
- Organizations (companies, government agencies, NGOs,
military, media outlets, groups)
- Locations (cities, regions, facilities, countries)

Requirements:
- Use only entities explicitly supported by the article text;
do not invent or infer entities.
- For each entity, include a short evidence excerpt from the
article showing why it was extracted.
```

```
- If an entity is ambiguous, mark it Ambiguous and explain why
using only article context; do not guess.

Output format (structured text):
People:
- Name | Role/descriptor (if stated) | Evidence excerpt |
Ambiguous? (Yes/No) | Ambiguity rationale (if applicable)
Organizations:
- Name | Type (or Unknown) | Evidence excerpt | Ambiguous? (Yes/
No) | Ambiguity rationale (if applicable)
Locations:
- Name | Type (city/region/facility/country) | Evidence excerpt |
Ambiguous? (Yes/No) | Ambiguity rationale (if applicable)

Article Title: {title}
Article URL: {url}
Article Text:
{article_text}
""".strip()
```

Developing an AI-Enhanced Python Script

With the Name Entity Recognition prompt defined, we can now integrate it into a working Python script. This script represents the first stage of actionable intelligence extraction: identifying people, organizations, and locations referenced within an article.

Rather than introducing complexity all at once, we begin by walking through the **main execution path** of the script. This approach makes it easier to understand how data flows from RSS ingestion to structured intelligence output. Supporting functions are introduced afterward, once their role in the pipeline is clear.

At a high level, the script performs the following steps:

1. Retrieve and parse an RSS feed

2. Select the most recent article entry

3. Extract basic metadata, including the article title, URL, and author

4. Download and parse the full article content using the Newspaper library

5. Build a Name Entity Recognition prompt using the article title, URL, and raw article text

6. Submit the prompt to OpenAI for processing

7. Parse the returned entity data into analyst-friendly tables

8. Display the results in a readable, structured format

This structure mirrors how an analyst would manually approach an article but automates the process in a repeatable and scalable way.

Main Script Execution Flow

The following code shows the primary execution block of the script. This section acts as the orchestration layer, coordinating RSS retrieval, article processing, AI-assisted extraction, and final presentation.

Note   Script 5-1 is available from the GitHub site for easy use and study

---

In this example, I chose the BBC Science and Environment RSS Feed for examination. The title of this article is "Supersized dump fire risk report kept from public".

```python
if __name__ == "__main__":
    # BBC Science and environment RSS Feed
    feedURL = "http://feeds.bbci.co.uk/news/science_and_environment/rss.xml"

    # Retrieve the contents of the feed
    feed = feedparser.parse(feedURL)
    # Only process valid feeds
    if feed:
        # Obtain the most recent feed entry
        entry = feed.entries[0]
        # Obtain the title, article url and author
        title  = entry.title
        url    = entry.link
        try:
            author = entry.author
        except:
            author = "Unknown"
        # download and parse the article
        article = Article(url)
        article.download()
        article.parse()
        # Obtain the article text
        nativeText = article.text

        # build the NER Prompt
        nerPrompt = BuildNERPrompt(title, url, nativeText)

        # Leverage OpenAI to process the prompt
        articleNER = OpenAIResponse(nerPrompt)

        # Parse the results and create tabularize results
        people, orgs, locations = ParseNERResults(articleNER)
        # print out the resulting tables
        print(people)
        print(orgs)
        print(locations)
```

Sample Output from Script 5-1

Before we examine the new functions BuildNERPrompt and
ParseNERResults let's look at the script output from the article "What are
critical minerals and why do countries need them?" As you can see, there
was only one person identified during the AI analysis of the article. The AI
analysis also identified organizations Highnam and EA. As you can see,
EA is identified as "Ambiguous" as the article uses an abbreviation without
defining it. Finally, the AI analysis identifies two locations mentioned:

labeling Highnam as "Ambiguous" as Highnam is only mentioned within the context of the Parish council and does not clearly define Highnam as a definite location.

```
+--------------------------------------------------------------------------------------------------------------+
|                                              People                                                           |
+--------+-----------------------------------+-------------------------------+-----------+---------+
| Name   | Role                              | Evidence                      | Ambiguous | Notes   |
+--------+-----------------------------------+-------------------------------+-----------+---------+
| Coats  | Chairman of Highnam Parish Council| "Coats, who is chairman of    | No        |         |
|        |                                   | Highnam Parish Council, said  |           |         |
|        |                                   | that while action was being   |           |         |
|        |                                   | taken over the Oxfordshire    |           |         |
|        |                                   | site..."                      |           |         |
+--------+-----------------------------------+-------------------------------+-----------+---------+
```

```
+--------------------------------------------------------------------------------------------------------------+
|                                           Organizations                                                      |
+-------------------------+-----------------------+-------------------------------------+-----------+-----------------------+
| Name                    | Type                  | Evidence                            | Ambiguous | Notes                 |
+-------------------------+-----------------------+-------------------------------------+-----------+-----------------------+
| Highnam Parish Council  | Local government      | "Coats, who is chairman of Highnam  | No        |                       |
|                         | council               | Parish Council"                     |           |                       |
+-------------------------+-----------------------+-------------------------------------+-----------+-----------------------+
| EA                      | Unknown (likely       | "its formal complaint to the EA,    | Yes       | The article uses the  |
|                         | Environmental Agency  | which, he said, was 'continually    |           | abbreviation "EA"     |
|                         | but not explicitly    | and blatantly' ignoring the         |           | without explicitly    |
|                         | stated)               | interests of the local community"   |           | defining it.          |
+-------------------------+-----------------------+-------------------------------------+-----------+-----------------------+
```

```
+--------------------------------------------------------------------------------------------------------------+
|                                              Locations                                                       |
+-------------+-----------------------+-----------------------------------+-----------+-----------------------------+
| Name        | Type                  | Evidence                          | Ambiguous | Notes                       |
+-------------+-----------------------+-----------------------------------+-----------+-----------------------------+
| Oxfordshire | Region                | "while action was being taken     | No        |                             |
|             |                       | over the Oxfordshire site"        |           |                             |
+-------------+-----------------------+-----------------------------------+-----------+-----------------------------+
| Highnam     | Ambiguous (likely a   | "Coats, who is chairman of        | Yes       | The article mentions        |
|             | place related to the  | Highnam Parish Council"           |           | Highnam only in the context |
|             | Parish Council but    |                                   |           | of the Parish Council; it   |
|             | not explicitly        |                                   |           | does not explicitly state   |
|             | stated as a           |                                   |           | that Highnam is a location. |
|             | location)             |                                   |           |                             |
+-------------+-----------------------+-----------------------------------+-----------+-----------------------------+
```

Building the NER Extraction Prompt

```python
def BuildNERPrompt(title, url, articleText):
    NERExtractionPrompt = f"""
    Examine the following article text and extract named entities.

    Identify:
    - People
    - Organizations (companies, government agencies, NGOs, military, media outlets, groups)
    - Locations (cities, regions, facilities, countries)

    Requirements:
    - Use only entities explicitly supported by the article text; do not invent or infer entities.
    - For each entity, include a short evidence excerpt from the article showing why it was extracted.
    - If an entity is ambiguous, mark it Ambiguous and explain why using only article context; do not guess.

    Output format (structured text):
    People:
    - Name | Role/descriptor (if stated) | Evidence excerpt | Ambiguous? (Yes/No) | Ambiguity rationale (if applicable)
    Organizations:
    - Name | Type (or Unknown) | Evidence excerpt | Ambiguous? (Yes/No) | Ambiguity rationale (if applicable)
    Locations:
    - Name | Type (city/region/facility/country) | Evidence excerpt | Ambiguous? (Yes/No) | Ambiguity rationale (if applicable)

    Article Title: {title}
    Article URL:   {url}
    Article Text:  {articleText}
    """
```

The BuildNERPrompt() function is responsible for converting an article
into a **well-scoped extraction task** that the AI model can execute reliably.
Rather than issuing a vague "find entities" request, this function constructs
a prompt that enforces discipline: it defines exactly what to extract, how to
justify each extraction, and how to format the results so they can be parsed
automatically.

This approach shifts complexity upstream. By designing a predictable
response format, we simplify downstream processing and reduce the
likelihood of hallucination or inconsistent output.

High-Level Function Behavior

At a high level, BuildNERPrompt() performs four key tasks:

1. **Define the Extraction Objective**

   The prompt starts by explicitly instructing the
   model to extract named entities from the article
   text. This narrows the task and reduces drift into
   summarization, opinion, or narrative rewriting.

2. **Specify Entity Categories**

    The function lists the three categories we care about
    for actionable intelligence extraction:

    - People

    - Organizations

    - Locations

    Organizations and locations are further clarified with examples
    (e.g., NGOs, military, facilities, countries) to reduce ambiguity
    and improve consistency across sources.

3. **Enforce Grounding and Uncertainty Handling**

    The prompt includes constraints designed to keep
    the output defensible:

    - Extract only what is explicitly supported by the
      article text

    - Provide evidence excerpts for each entity

    - Mark ambiguous entities and explain ambiguity
      using article context only

    - Avoid guessing

    These rules mirror professional investigative standards: results
    must be traceable and uncertainty must be explicit.

4. **Standardize Output Format for Automation**

    The prompt dictates a consistent, structured layout for the
    response (People, Organizations, Locations), and requires
    fields to be returned in a predictable order. This enables
    lightweight parsing and clean presentation (PrettyTable)
    without requiring complex Natural Language Processing
    (NLP) post-processing.

Parsing and Structuring NER Results

```python
def ParseNERResults(text):
    peopleTable, orgTable, loccationTable = CreateNERTables()
    current_section = None

    for line in text.splitlines():
        line = line.strip()

        if line.startswith("People:"):
            current_section = "people"
            continue
        elif line.startswith("Organizations:"):
            current_section = "orgs"
            continue
        elif line.startswith("Locations:"):
            current_section = "locations"
            continue

        if not line.startswith("-"):
            continue

        parts = [p.strip() for p in line.lstrip("-").split("|")]
        while len(parts) < 5:
            parts.append("")

        if current_section == "people":
            peopleTable.add_row(parts)
        elif current_section == "orgs":
            orgTable.add_row(parts)
        elif current_section == "locations":
            loccationTable.add_row(parts)

    return peopleTable, orgTable, loccationTable
```

The ParseNERResults() function is responsible for transforming the structured text returned by the AI model into analyst-friendly tabular output. Rather than attempting complex natural language parsing, this function assumes a **disciplined, predictable output format**, as defined by the NER extraction prompt.

This design choice is intentional. By controlling the prompt output, we dramatically simplify downstream processing.

ParseNERResults—High-Level Function Behavior

At a high level, ParseNERResults() performs four key tasks:

1. **Initialize Output Tables**

   The function begins by creating three PrettyTable
   objects one each for people, organizations, and
   locations. These tables define the final presentation
   format used throughout the chapter. (Note: We
   defined and provided examples of PrettyTables in
   previous chapters.)

```python
def CreateNERTables():
    people = PrettyTable()
    people.field_names = ["Name", "Role", "Evidence", "Ambiguous", "Notes"]

    orgs = PrettyTable()
    orgs.field_names = ["Name", "Type", "Evidence", "Ambiguous", "Notes"]

    locations = PrettyTable()
    locations.field_names = ["Name", "Type", "Evidence", "Ambiguous", "Notes"]

    for table in (people, orgs, locations):
        table.max_width["Evidence"] = 40
        table.max_width['Notes'] = 30
        if table == people:
            table.title = "People"
        elif table == orgs:
            table.title = "Organizations"
        elif table == locations:
            table.title = "Locations"
        table.align = 'l'
        table.hrules = ALL
        table.wrap = True

    return people, orgs, locations
```

2. **Track the Active Entity Section**

   As the function iterates through the AI-generated
   text line by line, it maintains awareness of the
   current entity section (People, Organizations, or
   Locations). Section headers in the output determine
   where subsequent entity rows should be placed.

3. **Extract and Normalize Entity Fields**

   Each entity entry is split into its component fields
   using a consistent delimiter. If fields are missing, the
   function pads the row to preserve table alignment.
   This normalization step ensures reliable output
   even when some entities contain less information
   than others.

4. **Populate the Appropriate Tables**

   Based on the active section, parsed rows are added
   to the corresponding PrettyTable. This produces
   clean, categorized results that are immediately
   readable and ready for reporting.

Interpreting Entity Results

From Entity Extraction to Entity Enrichment

Up to this point, we have focused on identifying named entities
within article: people, organizations, and locations. While extraction
provides structure, intelligence value emerges when we take the next step:
contextual enrichment.

In Chapter 4, we developed a method for profiling authors using
contextual grounding and attribution discipline. In this section, we
generalize that approach. Rather than limiting profiling to the article's
author, we extend the method to every entity discovered during Name
Entity Recognition. Notice the subtle changes to the NERPrompt
shown here.

```python
def BuildNERPrompt(title, url, articleText):
    NERExtractionPrompt = f"""
    Examine the following article text and extract named entities.

    Identify:
    - People
    - Organizations (companies, government agencies, NGOs, military, media outlets, groups)
    - Locations (cities, regions, facilities, countries)

    Requirements:
    - Use only entities explicitly supported by the article text; do not invent or infer entities.
    - For each entity, include a short evidence excerpt from the article showing why it was extracted.
    - If an entity is ambiguous, mark it Ambiguous and explain why using only article context; do not guess.

    Output format (structured text):
    People:
    - Name | Role/descriptor (if stated) |  Ambiguous? (Yes/No)
    Organizations:
    - Name | Type (or Unknown) | Ambiguous? (Yes/No)
    Locations:
    - Name | Type (city/region/facility/country) | Ambiguous? (Yes/No)

    Article Title: {title}
    Article URL:    {url}
    Article Text:   {articleText}
    """

    return NERExtractionPrompt.strip()
```

This transforms our workflow from simple entity identification to a scalable enrichment pipeline.

Generalizing the Profiling Method

- The profiling function introduced earlier was designed to

    - Anchor identity to authoritative source material

    - Prevent name collisions and improper merging

    - Explicitly label uncertainty

    - Produce simple text-based output for review

Notice that we have changed the profiling method below to include not only the name, but also the affiliations and confidence characteristics of our findings. This is subtle but important if we are to trust the results delivered by the LLM.

```python
def BuildProfilePrompt(name, association, articleText):
    prompt = f"""

Perform name attribution and background enrichment using the information below:

Name: "{name}"
Association: "{association}"
Article : "{articleText}"

Use the {articleText} as the authoritative source for Name and Association.

Follow these rules strictly:
1. Treat the {articleText} as the ground truth for name identity.
2. Do NOT merge information from authors with the same or similar names unless there is strong evidence they are the same.
3. If information cannot be confidently verified, state "unknown".
4. Do NOT invent contact information.

Produce a clear, human-readable name intelligence summary with the following sections:

Name:
Affiliation:
Background:
Attribution Confidence:

The output should be concise, professional, and suitable for inclusion in an investigative report.
"""

    return prompt.strip()
```

In this script, we repurpose that methodology for three entity categories:

- People

- Organizations

- Locations

Instead of treating each entity type differently, we apply the same disciplined enrichment framework across all categories. The result is consistent, defensible profiling output regardless of entity type.

Architectural Flow of Script 5-2

Note   Script 5-2 is available from the GitHub site for easy use and study.

Script 5-2 expands the original extraction pipeline into a two-stage intelligence workflow.

Stage 1: Extraction

Retrieve the RSS feed. Download and parse the full article. Normalize language (detect and translate if necessary). Build the NER extraction prompt. Our approach examines the article text for language used. If the article is in English, the native text is English. On the other hand, if the article is not written in English, we simply leverage OpenAI to translate the article for us.

```python
# download and parse the article
article = Article(url)
article.download()
article.parse()

# Obtain the article text
nativeText = article.text

languagePrompt = "Is the predominent language in this article English yes|no "+nativeText

ans = OpenAIResponse(languagePrompt)

if ans != "yes":
    englishText = OpenAIResponse("Translate this article to English "+nativeText)
else:
    englishText = nativeText

# build the NER Prompt
nerPrompt = BuildNERPrompt(title, url, englishText)

# Leverage OpenAI to process the prompt
articleNER = OpenAIResponse(nerPrompt)

# Parse the results and create tabularize results
peopleList, orgsList, locationsList = ParseNERResults(articleNER)
```

Submit to OpenAI and parse structured results into entity lists. At this point, we now have three Python lists:

- peopleList

- orgsList

- locationsList

Each list contains: Entity name, Associated descriptor or type, and an Ambiguity indicator. Extraction is now complete and structure has been imposed on unstructured text.

Stage 2: Enrichment

The next phase iterates over each extracted entity and applies a modified profiling prompt. For each entity, we

- Extract the name and association

- Build a profiling prompt using BuildProfilePrompt()

- Submit the prompt to OpenAI

- Print the structured intelligence summary

```python
# Parse the results and create tabularize results
peopleList, orgsList, locationsList = ParseNERResults(articleNER)

peopleTable = PrettyTable(["Name", "Affiliation", "Background", "Attribution Confidence"])
peopleTable.title = "People Results"
peopleTable.align = 'l'
peopleTable.max_width["Affiliation"] = 20
peopleTable.max_width["Background"] = 40
peopleTable.max_width["Attribution Confidence"] = 30
peopleTable.hrules = ALL
peopleTable.wrap = True

for eachName in peopleList:
    name = eachName[0]
    association = eachName[1]

    prompt = BuildProfilePrompt(name, association, url)

    nameProfile = OpenAIResponse(prompt)

    fields = parseProfile(nameProfile)

    peopleTable.add_row([fields["Name"], fields["Affiliation"], fields["Background"], fields["Attribution Confidence"]])

print(peopleTable.get_string())
```

The abbreviated tabular results of the AI Analysis are shown here in three sections: People Results, Organization Results, and Location Results. Each table provides the Name, the Known Affiliation, Background and Attribution Confidence. Notice the rich AI Analysis that is delivered.

```
+-------------------------------------------------------------------------------------------------------------+
|  I                                    People Results                                                         |
+-------+---------------------+------------------------------------------+------------------------------------+
| Name  | Affiliation         | Background                               | Attribution Confidence             |
+-------+---------------------+------------------------------------------+------------------------------------+
| Coats | Chairman of Highnam | Coats holds a leadership position within | High (based on the BBC article     |
|       | Parish Council      | the local government structure as the    | as the definitive source)          |
|       |                     | chairman of Highnam Parish Council.      |                                    |
|       |                     | Further personal or professional         |                                    |
|       |                     | background details are not provided in   |                                    |
|       |                     | the authoritative source.                |                                    |
+-------+---------------------+------------------------------------------+------------------------------------+
```

```
+------------------------------------------------------------------------------------------------------------------+
|                                          Organization Results                                                    |
+------------------------+----------------------+----------------------------------------+---------------------------+
| Name                   | Affiliation          | Background                             | Attribution Confidence    |
+------------------------+----------------------+----------------------------------------+---------------------------+
| Highnam Parish Council | Local government     | Highnam Parish Council is a local      | High (information directly |
|                        | council              | government body responsible for        | verified from the BBC News |
|                        |                      | representing the interests of the      | article at https://www.bbc.com |
|                        |                      | Highnam community. It operates at the  | /news/articles/c78x966g75xo?at |
|                        |                      | parish level, addressing local issues  | _medium=RSS&at_campaign=rss) |
|                        |                      | and governance within its jurisdiction.|                           |
|                        |                      | The council plays a role in community  |                           |
|                        |                      | planning, local services, and liaising |                           |
|                        |                      | with higher levels of government.      |                           |
+------------------------+----------------------+----------------------------------------+---------------------------+
| EA                     | Unknown              | The individual identified as "EA" is   | High (based on direct     |
|                        | (abbreviation not    | referenced in the BBC article (https://w | reference from the      |
|                        | expanded in source)  | ww.bbc.com/news/articles/c78x966g75xo?at | authoritative BBC article, |
|                        |                      | _medium=RSS&at_campaign=rss) without   | with no further identifying |
|                        |                      | further elaboration on their full name | information available)    |
|                        |                      | or organizational affiliation. No      |                           |
|                        |                      | additional biographical or professional|                           |
|                        |                      | details are provided within the source.|                           |
+------------------------+----------------------+----------------------------------------+---------------------------+
```

```
+------------------------------------------------------------------------------------------------------------------+
|                                          Location Results                                                        |
+----------------+----------------+--------------------------------------------------+--------------------------+
| Name           | Affiliation    | Background                                        | Attribution Confidence   |
+----------------+----------------+--------------------------------------------------+--------------------------+
| Oxfordshire    | Region         | Oxfordshire is a county located in               | High                     |
|                |                | South East England, known for its                |                          |
|                |                | historical significance, academic                |                          |
|                |                | institutions, and rural landscapes. The          |                          |
|                |                | region often features in news related to         |                          |
|                |                | local governance, development projects,          |                          |
|                |                | and community affairs. According to the          |                          |
|                |                | referenced BBC News article, Oxfordshire         |                          |
|                |                | is identified as a regional entity               |                          |
|                |                | involved in the context discussed,               |                          |
|                |                | reflecting its administrative and                |                          |
|                |                | geographical role within the UK.                 |                          |
+----------------+----------------+--------------------------------------------------+--------------------------+
```

This approach is intentionally iterative and modular. The profiling logic does not depend on how the entity was extracted; it only requires a name and contextual association.

Why This Matters: This enhancement introduces several important intelligence principles.

1. Separation of Concerns

- Extraction and enrichment are handled independently.

- If extraction improves, enrichment remains stable.

- If enrichment logic evolves, extraction does not need to change.

- This modularity makes the pipeline extensible for later chapters.

2. Context-Grounded Profiling

- The profiling prompt explicitly

  - Treats the article as ground truth

  - Prevents merging similar names without strong evidence

  - Prohibits invention of unverifiable details

  - Requires uncertainty to be declared

- This is critical in investigative workflows, where false attribution can have significant consequences.

3. Generalized Intelligence Framework

By modifying the author profiling method into a generalized enrichment function, we have effectively created a reusable intelligence module. The same prompt structure can now profile:

- A quoted executive

- A government agency

- A military unit

- A geographic region

The pipeline no longer cares whether the entity is a person, organization, institution, or location the process remains consistent.

Conceptual Shift: From Article to Entity Network

Using this methodology, the article is no longer the primary object of analysis. It becomes a source document feeding an entity intelligence system.

The workflow now resembles

RSS Feed → Article → Entity Extraction → Entity Lists → Entity Profiling → Intelligence Summaries

This is a fundamental shift. Instead of reading one article at a time, we are building structured intelligence around the actors referenced within it.

Foreign RSS Feed Example

Utilizing Scripts 5-1 and 5-2, I wanted to demonstrate a Foreign-Language RSS feed that has been translated into English and then processed to obtain details of People, Organizations, and Locations identified in the article. For this example, I used a German Security News RSS Feed:

"`https://www.heise.de/security/rss/news-atom.xml`".

The title of the article is provided in both English and German:

- IPFire introduces free domain blocklist DBL—English

- IPFire stellt freie Domain-Blockliste DBL vor—German

Here are the results of AI processing with Script 5-1, for People, Organizations, and Locations.

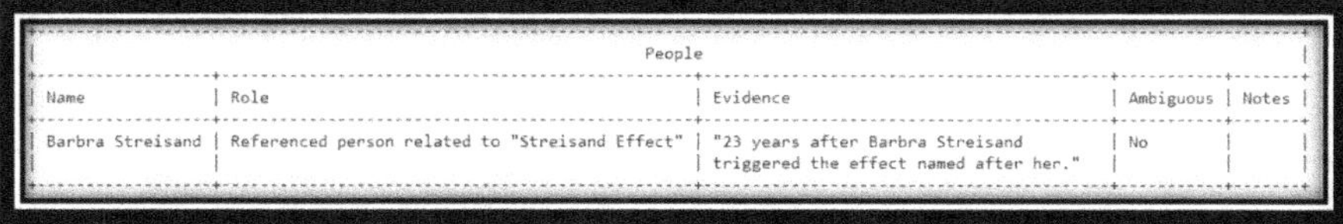

People				
Name	Role	Evidence	Ambiguous	Notes
Barbra Streisand	Referenced person related to "Streisand Effect"	"23 years after Barbra Streisand triggered the effect named after her."	No	

```
+-----------------------------------------------------------------------------------------------------------+
|                                            Organizations                                                  |
+--------------------------+----------------------+-----------------------------+-------------+-------------+
| Name                     | Type                 | Evidence                    | Ambiguous   | Notes       |
+--------------------------+----------------------+-----------------------------+-------------+-------------+
| Palantir Technologies    | Company (US provider | "Palantir Technologies, the US provider | No          |             |
|                          | of analytics         | of analytics software"      |             |             |
|                          | software)            |                             |             |             |
+--------------------------+----------------------+-----------------------------+-------------+-------------+
| Republik                 | Media outlet (Swiss  | "two reports from the Swiss online | No          |             |
|                          | online magazine)     | magazine 'Republik.'"       |             |             |
+--------------------------+----------------------+-----------------------------+-------------+-------------+
| Cantonal Superior Court  | Court (Swiss         | "the communications officer of the | No          |             |
|                          | judicial body)       | Cantonal Superior Court told heise |             |             |
|                          |                      | online"                     |             |             |
+--------------------------+----------------------+-----------------------------+-------------+-------------+
| Commercial Court of Zurich | Court (Swiss       | "The responsible court here is the | No          |             |
|                          | judicial body)       | Commercial Court of Zurich." |             |             |
+--------------------------+----------------------+-----------------------------+-------------+-------------+
```

```
+-----------------------------------------------------------------------------------------------------------+
|                                              Locations                                                    |
+--------------+----------+-------------------------------------------+-------------+---------+
| Name         | Type     | Evidence                                  | Ambiguous   | Notes   |
+--------------+----------+-------------------------------------------+-------------+---------+
| Switzerland  | Country  | "the company has so far - as far as       | No          |         |
|              |          | known - had little state clientele in     |             |         |
|              |          | Switzerland."                             |             |         |
+--------------+----------+-------------------------------------------+-------------+---------+
| Germany      | Country  | "While in Germany, the provider of data   | No          |         |
|              |          | linking and data analysis software for    |             |         |
|              |          | authorities with surveillance powers is   |             |         |
|              |          | at least successful with some government  |             |         |
|              |          | customers"                                |             |         |
+--------------+----------+-------------------------------------------+-------------+---------+
| USA          | Country  | "In its home market, the USA, the         | No          |         |
|              |          | company does about a quarter of a         |             |         |
|              |          | billion US dollars in business"           |             |         |
+--------------+----------+-------------------------------------------+-------------+---------+
```

Here is the result of AI processing with Script 5-2 for People, Organizations, and Locations.

```
+-----------------------------------------------------------------------------------------------------------+
|                                            People Results                                                 |
+-------------------+------------------------+------------------------------------------+------------------------+
| Name              | Affiliation            | Background                               | Attribution Confidence |
+-------------------+------------------------+------------------------------------------+------------------------+
| Barbra Streisand  | Referenced as the origin of | Barbra Streisand is known primarily as | High (based on the       |
|                   | the "Streisand Effect" | the namesake of the "Streisand Effect,"  | authoritative source h   |
|                   |                        | a phenomenon where attempts to suppress  | ttps://www.heise.de/ne   |
|                   |                        | information inadvertently lead to        | ws/Palantir-gegen-die-   |
|                   |                        | greater public exposure. This           | Republik-US-             |
|                   |                        | association is cited in the context of   | Analysefirma-geht-       |
|                   |                        | legal and information control disputes,  | gegen-Magazin-vor-       |
|                   |                        | as referenced in the article concerning  | Gericht-11176503.html)   |
|                   |                        | Palantir's legal actions against a       |                          |
|                   |                        | magazine. Further personal or            |                          |
|                   |                        | professional details are not provided in |                          |
|                   |                        | the source.                              |                          |
+-------------------+------------------------+------------------------------------------+------------------------+
```

Organization Results			
Name	Affiliation	Background	Attribution Confidence
Palantir Technologies	Company (US provider of analytics software)	Palantir Technologies is a US-based company specializing in analytics software. The firm is known for providing data integration and analysis solutions, often used by government agencies and private sector clients for complex data-driven decision-making. According to the referenced article from Heise Online, Palantir has recently engaged in legal action against a magazine, highlighting its active role in protecting its corporate interests and public image.	High (based on authoritative source from Heise Online)
Republik	Media outlet (Swiss online magazine)	Republik is a Swiss online magazine known for its investigative journalism. It has gained attention for in-depth reporting and critical coverage on various topics, including legal disputes involving major corporations. Recently, the U.S.-based data analytics firm Palantir initiated legal action against Republik, highlighting the magazine's role in scrutinizing powerful entities.	High (based on the authoritative article from heise.de)
Commercial Court of Zurich	Court (judicial body)	The Commercial Court of Zurich is a judicial body referenced in the context of a legal dispute involving the US analysis firm Palantir and the Swiss magazine Republik. It serves as the venue where Palantir initiated legal proceedings against the magazine, indicating the court's role in adjudicating commercial and related legal matters within Zurich.	High (based on the authoritative source https://www.heise.de/news/Palantir-gegen-die-Republik-US-Analysefirma-geht-gegen-Magazin-vor-Gericht-11176503.html)
US federal agencies	Government agencies (USA)	US federal agencies refer to the various governmental bodies operating under the United States federal government. These agencies are responsible for implementing and enforcing federal laws, regulations, and policies across diverse sectors including national security, law enforcement, public health, and more. The referenced article highlights interactions involving these agencies in the context of legal and surveillance activities, specifically relating to the US analysis firm Palantir and its legal actions against a magazine.	High (based on the authoritative source provided)

Location Results			
Name	Affiliation	Background	Attribution Confidence
Switzerland	Country	Switzerland is a sovereign nation in Central Europe known for its political neutrality, strong economy, and high standard of living. The referenced article from Heise discusses legal actions involving the US analytics firm Palantir but does not provide additional specific details about Switzerland itself. Therefore, no further background information beyond its status as a country can be confidently attributed from the source.	High (based on authoritative source)
Germany	Country	Germany is a sovereign nation in Central Europe known for its significant political, economic, and cultural influence within the European Union and globally. The referenced article discusses legal actions involving the US analytics firm Palantir and a German magazine, highlighting Germany's role as the jurisdiction where this dispute unfolds, reflecting its active legal and media landscape.	High (based on authoritative source)

Zurich	City (implied by "Commercial Court of Zurich")	Zurich is referenced in the context of the "Commercial Court of Zurich," indicating its role as a jurisdictional entity associated with legal proceedings. The city is mentioned in relation to a court case involving the US analysis firm Palantir and the magazine "Republik," as reported by the article from Heise Online. This establishes Zurich as a key location for the legal dispute described.	High (based on explicit mention in the authoritative source)
USA	Country	The United States of America (USA) is a federal republic primarily located in North America, consisting of 50 states and a federal district. It is a major global political, economic, and military power. The referenced article discusses a legal dispute involving Palantir, a US-based data analytics company, highlighting the country context in which this corporate and legal activity takes place.	High (based on authoritative source)

Limitations, Bias, and Validation

Trust, but Verify is a critical posture we need to follow:

- We must know and respect the limitations of AI-driven NER.

- Consider possible false positives and over-extraction.

- We must avoid cultural and linguistic bias.

Summary

This chapter marked a critical transition in our intelligence pipeline: the shift from processing content to extracting structure. While previous chapters focused on acquiring RSS feeds, normalizing multilingual text, and profiling authors, this chapter expanded the scope of analysis to include every meaningful actor referenced within an article.

We began by reframing the purpose of reading. A media reporter reads to inform. A digital forensic investigator reads to corroborate. An intelligence analyst reads to uncover structure. Through this lens, articles are no longer static narratives but become rich sources of interconnected entities. Name Entity Recognition (NER) serves as the mechanism that enables this transformation, allowing us to systematically identify people, organizations, and locations that form the backbone of operational context.

We examined which entities matter and why. People beyond the author often signal influence, decision-making authority, or emerging actors. Organizations reveal alignment, power structures, and recurring institutional involvement. Locations provide geographic signals that may indicate strategic importance, escalation zones, or areas of repeated activity. Importantly, we emphasized that intelligence value does not require perfect extraction only consistent extraction. When applied across large volumes of content, repeatable entity identification reveals patterns that individual articles alone cannot.

From a technical perspective, we demonstrated how disciplined prompt design reduces hallucination, enforces grounding, and standardizes output for automation. By shifting complexity upstream defining clear extraction objectives, structured response formats, and ambiguity handling rules, we simplified downstream parsing and presentation. The separation of extraction and enrichment introduced modularity into the pipeline, allowing us to first identify entities and then selectively profile them using a generalized attribution framework.

This progression culminated in Script 5-2, where extraction evolved into enrichment. By adapting the author profiling methodology from Chapter 4 into a generalized entity profiling engine, we created a scalable intelligence module capable of producing contextual summaries for people, organizations, and locations alike. The article itself became a feeder document into a broader entity intelligence system:

RSS Feed → Article → Entity Extraction → Entity Lists → Entity Profiling → Intelligence Summaries

At this stage, the workflow no longer revolves around reading one article at a time. Instead, it constructs structured, traceable intelligence around the actors embedded within the narrative.

Finally, we acknowledged the limitations of AI-assisted NER. Ambiguity, aliasing, transliteration differences, abbreviation conflicts, and cultural bias remain important considerations. Effective intelligence automation requires discipline, validation, and a "trust, but verify" posture.

This chapter established the structural foundation for actionable intelligence extraction. We now possess a repeatable method for identifying who is involved, where activity occurs, and how entities relate to one another. Yet identification alone is insufficient. To fully assess impact and risk, we must evaluate tone, intent, urgency, and contextual significance.

Looking Ahead to Chapter 6: From Entities to Deeper Sentiment and Threat Analysis

Chapter 5 established the structural foundation of intelligence extraction. We identified entities, grounded them in evidence, and enriched them with contextual background. The article is no longer just text; it is a network of actors and affiliations.

However, intelligence without interpretation is incomplete. Entities tell us who and where. Sentiment and relevance tell us why it matters. Tone can signal escalation. Language can reveal intent. AI examinations without carefully structured prompts can expose bias, urgency, hallucinations, false positives or improper conclusions.

In Chapter 6, we introduce sentiment and threat analysis, extending our pipeline to evaluate political, global, and social significance. The workflow now shifts from entity awareness to risk awareness transforming structured data into actionable insight.

Sentiment and Threat Analysis in OSINT

This is where OSINT becomes predictive rather than reactive.

Up to this point, we have focused on acquiring, cleaning, translating, and structuring information from RSS feeds and external sources. We have extracted entities, profiled authors, enriched context, and prepared our data for deeper interpretation. The next critical step is to move toward actionable intelligence.

In this chapter, we introduce two powerful analytical capabilities: **Sentiment Analysis** and **Threat Analysis**.

While previous chapters helped us understand *what* was said and *who* said it, this chapter focuses on *how it was said* and *whether it represents risk*.

In the context of OSINT, sentiment and threat evaluation are not academic exercises. They are essential capabilities for identifying emerging instability, tracking adversarial narratives, detecting coordinated campaigns, assessing geopolitical shifts, and recognizing signals of operational or physical risk. When properly implemented using Python and AI, these analytical layers elevate RSS processing from passive monitoring to proactive intelligence generation.

© Chet Hosmer 2026

C. Hosmer, *Extracting Intelligence from RSS News Feeds Using Python and AI*,
https://doi.org/10.1007/979-8-8688-2773-0_6

By the end of this chapter, you will be able to

- Automatically classify tone and emotional polarity in multilingual content

- Detect escalation language and indicators of hostility

- Identify potential operational threats within feed content

- Combine structured entities with sentiment and threat scoring

Sentiment Analysis in OSINT

What Is Sentiment Analysis?

- Definition: Computational identification of emotional tone.

- Polarity (Positive/Neutral/Negative).

- Emotional categories (including anger, fear, optimism, hostility, etc.).

- We need to examine linguistic signals vs. contextual signals.

- We need to apply AI-driven contextual sentiment vs. keyword-centric scoring.

Why Sentiment Analysis Matters in OSINT

In OSINT, sentiment analysis helps to

- Detect rising hostility toward individuals, organizations, or nations

- Identify narrative shifts in media ecosystems

- Track public reaction to events

- Detect coordinated information operations

- Monitor radicalization patterns

- Recognize early warning signs of civil unrest

- Assess tone in foreign-language reporting after translation

Analyzing Sentiment in RSS Articles: Basic Approach

As we have done in the past, we first start by retrieving article title and content. We then normalize and translate the article when needed and utilize AI to assess sentiment. It is important to note we are not only interested in the overall sentiment, but we also want a breakdown by sections to reveal where sentiment changes, what the detailed sentiment is, and specifically why this AI judgement was made.

Let's develop a new script that demonstrates how we can do this with Python, AI, and crafted prompts. Then we can apply this to an example article and examine the results.

Script 6-1 Analyzing Sentiment

When analyzing the sentiment of an article, it is important to develop a prompt that obtains detailed critical sentiment not just a positive or negative result without details. Therefore, as with previous chapters, the development of a comprehensive prompt is critical. Here is the Sentiment Analysis Prompt we have created in Python. We are using a function to develop the prompt; this allows you to expand or refine the prompt as needed. In this case, we direct the LLM to evaluate the sentiment in the context of OSINT analysis. We then specify the analysis categories as follows:

1. **Tone and Overall Sentiment**: Represent the general attitude and emotional direction conveyed by the article. This is a high-level classification that reflects how the subject matter is framed.

   a. **Positive**: Indicates optimism, progress, or favorable outcomes

   b. **Negative**: Reflects concern, criticism, or adverse implications

   c. **Neutral**: Presents information in a balanced, objective manner

2. **Primary Emotion**: Primary Emotion identifies the dominant emotional signal expressed in the content. While multiple emotions may be present, this category captures the most prominent examples including

   a. Fear

   b. Anger

   c. Joy

    d.   Sadness

    e.   Surprise

    f.   Trust

3. **Positive Sentiments**: Positive Sentiments are specific elements within the content that convey favorable or constructive perspectives. These may include

    a.   Expressions of success, progress, or innovation

    b.   Statements of support or approval

    c.   Indicators of stability or improvement

4. **Negative Sentiments**: Negative Sentiments highlight elements that reflect concern, risk, or unfavorable developments. These may include

    a.   Criticism or opposition

    b.   Indicators of failure, disruption, or decline

    c.   Warnings or expressions of uncertainty

5. **Neutral Sentiments**: Neutral Sentiments refer to content that is informational and lacks strong emotional or opinion-based language.

    a.   Fact-based reporting

    b.   Descriptive statements without judgment

    c.   Objective presentation of events or data

6. **Informative Sentiments**: Informative Sentiments capture the degree to which the content provides useful, actionable, or context-rich information, regardless of emotional tone.

    a.   Data-driven insights

    b.   Expert analysis or technical details

    c.   Context that enhances understanding of the topic

Note   This category is particularly important in OSINT, where informational value may outweigh emotional tone.

---

7. **Emotional Impacts**: Emotional Impacts describe the potential effect of the content on the reader or audience. This goes beyond what is expressed to consider what is *evoked*.
   Examples include

    a.   Inducing concern or urgency

    b.   Building confidence or reassurance

    c.   Provoking curiosity or further investigation

8. **Emotional Intensity**: Emotional Intensity measures the strength or magnitude of the emotions conveyed in the content.

    a.   **Low Intensity**: Minimal emotional language; largely factual

    b.   **Moderate Intensity**: Noticeable emotional cues but balanced with information

    c.   **High Intensity**: Strong, persuasive, or emotionally charged language

Below is the actual Python function that creates the prompt.

```python
def BuildSentimentPrompt(articleText):

    sentimentPrompt = f"""
    You are an intelligence analyst.

    Objective:
    Evaluate the sentiment of the following the {articleText} in the context of OSINT analysis.

    Instructions:
    1. Provide a detailed sentiment analysis of this article
    2. Provide an Emotional_Intensity score from 1 (low) to 5 (high).
    3. Identify the Primary_Emotion (e.g., Fear, Anger, Optimism, Hostility, Concern).

    Return your response ONLY in the following format:

    Return your response ONLY in the following format:

    Tone and Overall Sentiment:
    Positive Sentiments:
    Negative Sentiments:
    Neutral Sentiments:
    Informative Sentiments:
    Emotional Impacts:
    Emotional_Intensity:

    """

    return sentimentPrompt.strip()
```

Next, we create the main section of the script as shown here. Note you will see that I specified the 14th article in the chain of articles. When reviewing the titles of articles available, I found the 14th article of most interest as it was directly related to AI-powered cyber attacks. I created a script that allows me to peek at the list of articles that are available from a specific feed. I will, of course, provide that script later in the book.

```
+-------+------------------------------------------------------------------------------+
| Entry | Title                                                                        |
+-------+------------------------------------------------------------------------------+
| 0     | Darktrace Flags 32 Million Phishing Emails in 2025 as Identity Attacks Intensify |
| 1     | Exploitable Vulnerabilities Present in 87% of Organizations                  |
| 2     | UK's Data Watchdog Gets a Makeover to Match Growing Demands                  |
| 3     | Google Disrupts 'Prolific' and 'Elusive' China-Linked Global Hacking Campaign |
| 4     | Global Cyber Agencies Urge Immediate Patching of Cisco SD-WAN Zero Day       |
| 5     | 44% Surge in App Exploits as AI Speeds Up Cyber-Attacks, IBM Finds           |
| 6     | Malicious NuGet Package Targets Stripe Developers                           |
| 7     | Former Defense Contractor Boss Gets 7+ Years for Selling Zero Days           |
| 8     | ICO's £14m Reddit Fine Highlights Age Check Privacy Concerns                 |
| 9     | Cost of Insider Incidents Surges 20% to Nearly $20m                          |
| 10    | Multifaceted Phishing Scheme Deceives Bitpanda Customers                     |
| 11    | North Korean Lazarus Group Expands Ransomware Activity With Medusa           |
| 12    | AI Accelerates Attacker Breakout Time to Just Four Minutes                   |
| 13    | Chinese AI Firms Hit Claude with Distillation Attacks, Anthropic Warns       |
| 14    | AI-powered Cyber-Attacks Up Significantly in the Last Year, Warns CrowdStrike |
| 15    | Shai-Hulud-Like Worm Targets Developers via npm and AI Tools                 |
+-------+------------------------------------------------------------------------------+
```

```python
if __name__ == "__main__":

    # infosecurity Magazine Feed
    feedURL = "https://www.infosecurity-magazine.com/rss/news/"

    # Retrieve the contents of the feed
    feed = feedparser.parse(feedURL)

    # Only process valid feeds
    if feed:

        # Obtain the most recent feed entry
        entry = feed.entries[14]

        # Obtain the title, article url and author
        title   = entry.title
        url     = entry.link

        # download and parse the article
        article = Article(url)
        article.download()
        article.parse()

        # Obtain the article text
        articleText = article.text

        # build the Sentiment Prompt
        sentimentPrompt = BuildSentimentPrompt(articleText)

        # Leverage OpenAI to process the prompt
        sentimentDetails = OpenAIResponse(sentimentPrompt)

        print("Article Sentiment Analysis")
        print("Title:    ", title)
        print("URL:      ", url)
        print("\nSentiment:", sentimentDetails)
```

Sentiment Script 6-1 Sample Output English Article

The following English language article "AI-powered Cyber-Attacks Up Significantly in the Last Year, Warns CrowdStrike" was obtained from Infosecurity Magazine and is certainly relevant and related to this book and demonstrates a broad range of sentiment types.

```
                                    AI Sentiment-Analysis
-------------------------------------------------------------------------------------------------
 Category                     | Details
-------------------------------------------------------------------------------------------------
 Article:                     | The title "AI-powered Cyber-Attacks Up Significantly in the Last Year, Warns CrowdStrike" is already in English.
-------------------------------------------------------------------------------------------------
 URL:                         | https://www.infosecurity-magazine.com/news/ai-powered-cyberattacks-up/
-------------------------------------------------------------------------------------------------
 Tone and Overall Sentiment:  | The tone of the article is cautionary and analytical, with a focus on raising awareness about the increasing use of AI
                              | by malicious actors in cyber-attacks. The overall sentiment is predominantly negative due to the highlighting of threats
                              | and risks, but it remains factual and measured without sensationalism.
-------------------------------------------------------------------------------------------------
 Primary Emotion:             | Concern
-------------------------------------------------------------------------------------------------
 Positive Sentiments:         | - The article acknowledges that AI is currently used mainly to optimize existing attack methods rather than creating
                              | entirely new attack vectors, implying some limits to AI's threat potential at present.   - The detailed examples and
                              | research show that cybersecurity experts are actively monitoring and understanding these evolving threats.   - The
                              | report serves as an early warning, which could help organizations better prepare and defend against AI-enabled cyber
                              | threats.
-------------------------------------------------------------------------------------------------
 Negative Sentiments:         | - There is a significant increase (89%) in AI-enabled cyber-attacks, indicating growing threats.   - Use of AI by state-
                              | backed and criminal hacking groups to enhance phishing, malware, and espionage campaigns.   - AI tools are used to
                              | bypass safeguards, scale operations, and create more convincing malicious content.   - The embedding of LLMs in malware
                              | for operational tasks shows a dangerous evolution in attack sophistication.   - The article highlights the exploitation
                              | of AI for disinformation and intelligence gathering, which poses broader geopolitical risks.
-------------------------------------------------------------------------------------------------
 Neutral Sentiments:          | - The article provides factual reporting on the findings of the CrowdStrike Global Threat Report 2026.   - It notes that
                              | AI is currently a development aid rather than a revolutionary factor in cyber-attack effectiveness.   - Quotes from
                              | CrowdStrike experts provide context without emotional bias.
-------------------------------------------------------------------------------------------------
 Informative Sentiments:      | - The article is rich in specific examples (Chinese intelligence, Russian groups, Fancy Bear) illustrating AI's role in
                              | cyber threats.   - It explains the practical applications of AI in social engineering, malware development, and phishing
                              | campaigns.   - It highlights ongoing trends and anticipates future developments in AI-enabled cybercrime.
-------------------------------------------------------------------------------------------------
 Emotional Impacts:           | - The article may evoke concern or unease among readers about the growing sophistication and scale of cyber threats.   -
                              | It may raise awareness and vigilance among cybersecurity professionals and organizations.   - The measured tone helps
                              | prevent panic while emphasizing the seriousness of the issue.
-------------------------------------------------------------------------------------------------
```

Sentiment Script 6-1 Sample Output German Article

To demonstrate sentiment analysis on a foreign article, here are the results from a German security article translated to English. Note the title and article are translated. This is easily accomplished by changing the feed within the main function. Again, this article demonstrates the broad use of AI as a dangerous offensive technology.

```python
if __name__ == "__main__":

    # infosecurity Magazine Feed
    #feedURL = "https://www.infosecurity-magazine.com/rss/news/"
    feedURL = "https://www.heise.de/security/rss/news-atom.xml"
```

AI Sentiment-Analysis	
Category	Details
Article:	Claude: AI chatbot used for cyberattack on Mexican government
URL:	https://www.heise.de/news/Claude-KI-Chatbot-fuer-Cyberangriff-auf-mexikanische-Regierung-genutzt-11198396.html
Tone and Overall Sentiment:	The tone of the article is predominantly serious and cautionary, focusing on the gravity of a sophisticated cyberattack facilitated by AI tools. The overall sentiment is largely negative due to the exposure of sensitive government data and the implications for cybersecurity. However, there are some neutral and slightly positive elements related to the investigation and the efforts by AI companies to mitigate abuse.
Primary Emotion:	Concern
Positive Sentiments:	- Anthropic and OpenAI are actively investigating the incident and have taken measures such as suspending involved accounts. - AI developers are learning from malicious activities to improve safeguards in newer models (e.g., Claude Opus 4.6). - Transparency in reporting and technical editorial review of the article itself.
Negative Sentiments:	- A cybercriminal successfully exploited AI chatbots to infiltrate multiple Mexican government agencies. - Massive amounts of sensitive data, including taxpayer and voter information, were stolen. - The attack lasted about a month, indicating a prolonged breach. - Uncertainty remains about the identity of the attacker and the full scope of the damage. - The chatbot initially resisted but eventually complied with malicious commands, highlighting vulnerabilities in AI systems.
Neutral Sentiments:	- The article reports facts and findings from Bloomberg and Gambit Security without sensationalism. - Statements from involved companies and government agencies are presented without bias. - The mention that Gambit does not believe a foreign government is involved.
Informative Sentiments:	- Detailed description of how AI chatbots were used to detect vulnerabilities and automate data theft. - Explanation of the investigation status and responses from Anthropic and OpenAI. - Context on the scale of the data breach and affected institutions. - Insight into AI model improvements aimed at preventing misuse.
Emotional Impacts:	- The article likely evokes concern and unease about cybersecurity threats and the potential misuse of AI technologies. - It raises awareness of the challenges in securing sensitive government data in the digital age. - The cautious tone may instill a sense of vigilance regarding AI's dual-use potential.

What Are the Risks and Limitations of Sentiment Analysis

- AI Sarcasm detection difficulty.

- Misunderstanding of Cultural context issues.

- When articles are translated, bias may exist.

- In some cases, AI may blend News vs. Opinion.

- Neutral news about violent events may be misclassified as negative.

Threat Analysis in OSINT

What Is Threat Analysis?

Threat analysis examines articles to determine whether the content indicates

- Cyber threats

- Physical threats

- Political instability

- Infrastructure risk

- Economic disruption

- Coordinated influence operations

- Emerging vulnerabilities

Differentiate between

- Emotional negativity (sentiment)

- Actionable threat indicators

Why Threat Analysis Is Critical to OSINT

In the OSINT world:

- Threat signals often appear first in open media

- Exploit announcements can precede weaponization

- Political rhetoric precedes sanctions or conflict

- Cyber vulnerability typically precedes attacks

- Civil unrest signals appear before events

When examining ICS/OT threats:

- Infrastructure threats often surface in niche reporting

- Regulatory or vulnerability notices may indicate exposure or risk

- Adversarial actors may signal intentions publicly

Analyzing Threats in RSS Articles—Basic Approach

As we have done in the past, we first start by retrieving the article title and content. We then normalize and translate the article when needed and utilize AI to assess threats. It is important to note we are not only interested in the overall threat, but we also want a breakdown by sections to reveal where sentiment changes, what the detailed threat is, and specifically why this AI judgment was made.

Let's develop a new script that demonstrates how we can do this with Python, AI, and crafted prompts. Then we can apply this to an example article and examine the results.

Script 6-2 Analyzing Threat

When analyzing threats within an article, it is important to develop a prompt that obtains critical threat details not just a positive or negative result without details. Therefore, as with previous chapters the development of a comprehensive prompt is critical. Here is the Threat Analysis Prompt we have created in Python. We are using a function to develop the prompt; this allows you to expand or refine the prompt as needed. In this case, we direct the LLM to evaluate the threat in the context of OSINT analysis. We then specify the analysis categories as follows:

1. Overall, Threat Level

2. Threat Type

3. Urgency

4. Decision

5. Confidence

6. Reason

Below is the actual Python function that creates the Threat prompt followed by the main loop of the script. Note, I selected the same RSS Feed article for Threat as with the Sentiment example.

```python
def BuildThreatPrompt(articleText):

    threatPrompt = f"""
    You are a cybersecurity and geopolitical intelligence analyst.

    Objective:
    Determine whether the following article {articleText} represents a credible and
    actionable threat in an OSINT monitoring environment.

    Instructions:
    1. Provide a detailed threat analysis of this article
    2. Identify Threat_Type as one of:
       Cyber, Physical, Political, Economic, Informational, Infrastructure.
    3. Assign a Threat_Level from 0 (no threat) to 5 (critical threat).
    3. Identify urgency as:
       Immediate, Near-Term, Long-Term, or None.
    4. Provide a Decision:
       ESCALATE, MONITOR, or IGNORE.
    5. Provide a Confidence level:
       Low, Moderate, High.

    Return your response ONLY in the following format:

    Overall Threat Level:
    Threat Type:
    Urgency:
    Decision:
    Confidence:
    Rationale:

    """

    return threatPrompt.strip()
```

```python
if __name__ == "__main__":

    # infosecurity Magazine Feed
    feedURL = "https://www.infosecurity-magazine.com/rss/news/"

    # Retrieve the contents of the feed
    feed = feedparser.parse(feedURL)

    # Only process valid feeds
    if feed:

        # Obtain the most recent feed entry
        entry = feed.entries[15]

        # Obtain the title, article url and author
        title  = entry.title
        url    = entry.link

        # download and parse the article
        article = Article(url)
        article.download()
        article.parse()

        # Obtain the article text
        articleText = article.text

        # build the Threat Prompt
        threatPrompt = BuildThreatPrompt(articleText)

        # Leverage OpenAI to process the prompt
        threatDetails = OpenAIResponse(threatPrompt)

        print("Article Threat Analysis")
        print("Title:    ", title)
        print("URL:      ", url)
        print("\nThreat:", threatDetails)
```

Threat Script 6-2 Sample Output

English Article

Here is the resulting script output using the sample "AI-powered Cyber-Attacks Up Significantly in the Last Year, Warns CrowdStrike" article.

```
+------------------------------------------------------------------------------------------+
|                                   AI Threat-Analysis                                      |
+------------------------+-----------------------------------------------------------------+
| Category               | Details                                                         |
+------------------------+-----------------------------------------------------------------+
| Article:               | The title translates to English as:                             |
|                        | "AI-powered Cyber-Attacks Up Significantly in the Last Year, Warns CrowdStrike" |
+------------------------+-----------------------------------------------------------------+
| URL:                   | https://www.infosecurity-magazine.com/news/ai-powered-cyberattacks-up/ |
+------------------------+-----------------------------------------------------------------+
| Overall Threat Level   | 4                                                               |
+------------------------+-----------------------------------------------------------------+
| Threat Type            | Cyber, Informational                                           |
+------------------------+-----------------------------------------------------------------+
| Urgency                | Near-Term                                                       |
+------------------------+-----------------------------------------------------------------+
| Decision               | ESCALATE                                                       |
+------------------------+-----------------------------------------------------------------+
| Confidence             | High                                                           |
+------------------------+-----------------------------------------------------------------+
| Rationale              | High                                                           |
+------------------------+-----------------------------------------------------------------+
| Rationale              | The article highlights a significant and rapidly evolving threat landscape where |
|                        | AI and Large Language Models (LLMs) are increasingly weaponized by sophisticated |
|                        | threat actors, including state-backed groups. The reported 89% increase in AI- |
|                        | enabled cyber-attacks within a single year signals a sharp acceleration in |
|                        | adversaries' capabilities to scale and optimize traditional cyber-attack |
|                        | techniques, such as phishing, social engineering, and malware development. This |
|                        | trend represents a clear and growing cyber threat that directly impacts the |
|                        | confidentiality, integrity, and availability of information systems, |
|                        | particularly those tied to government, critical infrastructure, and private |
|                        | sector targets.                                                 |
+------------------------+-----------------------------------------------------------------+
```

Threat Script 6-2 Sample Output

German Article

```
+----------------------------+---------------------------------------------------------------+
|                            AI Threat-Analysis                                              |
+----------------------------+---------------------------------------------------------------+
| Category                   | Details                                                       |
+----------------------------+---------------------------------------------------------------+
| Article:                   | Claude: AI chatbot used for cyberattack on Mexican government  |
+----------------------------+---------------------------------------------------------------+
| URL:                       | https://www.heise.de/news/Claude-KI-Chatbot-fuer-Cyberangriff-auf-mexikanische- |
|                            | Regierung-genutzt-11190396.html                               |
+----------------------------+---------------------------------------------------------------+
| Overall Threat Level       | 4                                                             |
+----------------------------+---------------------------------------------------------------+
| Threat Type                | Cyber                                                         |
+----------------------------+---------------------------------------------------------------+
| Urgency                    | Immediate                                                     |
+----------------------------+---------------------------------------------------------------+
| Decision                   | ESCALATE                                                      |
+----------------------------+---------------------------------------------------------------+
| Confidence                 | High                                                         |
+----------------------------+---------------------------------------------------------------+
| Rationale                  | High                                                         |
+----------------------------+---------------------------------------------------------------+
| Rationale                  | This article describes a significant cyberattack leveraging AI chatbots to |
|                            | infiltrate multiple Mexican government networks, including highly sensitive |
|                            | agencies such as the Federal Tax Authority and the National Electoral Institute. |
|                            | The theft of 150 gigabytes of data, encompassing 195 million taxpayer records, |
|                            | voter information, government employee credentials, and registry files, |
|                            | constitutes a major breach of critical government infrastructure and personal |
|                            | data. Such a breach poses severe risks to national security, citizen privacy, |
|                            | and the integrity of electoral and tax systems. |
+----------------------------+---------------------------------------------------------------+
```

Differentiating Sentiment vs. Threat

As we examine both Sentiment and Threat you might ask what the key differences are. Here are some basic differences and use cases for each:

Sentiment	Threat
Measures tone	Measures risk
Emotional polarity	Operational consequence
Subjective	Action oriented
Provides trend analysis	Provides escalation and decisions

Chapter Implications

Sentiment and Threat Analysis in OSINT

This chapter marks a pivotal transition in the book moving from structured data extraction to structured intelligence evaluation. In earlier chapters, the focus was on acquiring RSS feeds, cleaning and normalizing multilingual content, extracting entities, profiling authors, and enriching contextual metadata. This chapter advances the system beyond information processing and into actionable intelligence generation.

The chapter introduces two foundational analytical layers: **Sentiment Analysis** and **Threat Analysis**. While previous work addressed *what was said* and *who said it*, this chapter concentrates on *how it was said* and *whether it represents risk*. This distinction is central to OSINT operations, where tone shifts and early warning indicators often precede operational events.

Sentiment Analysis As an Intelligence Signal

The chapter begins by defining sentiment analysis as the computational identification of emotional tone, including polarity (positive, neutral, negative) and emotional drivers such as concern, hostility, optimism, or fear. Importantly, the discussion moves beyond simple keyword-based scoring and emphasizes contextual AI-driven interpretation. Linguistic signals alone are insufficient in multilingual and nuanced reporting environments; contextual reasoning is required.

Positioning sentiment analysis not as an academic classification exercise but as a strategic OSINT capability. It enables analysts to

- Detect rising hostility toward organizations or nations

- Identify narrative shifts within media ecosystems

- Track emotional escalation in geopolitical reporting

- Monitor radicalization patterns

- Recognize early warning indicators of civil unrest

- Assess tone changes in translated foreign-language articles

The chapter reinforces that tone escalation can precede operational escalation, making sentiment tracking a predictive capability rather than a descriptive one.

From a technical standpoint, the chapter demonstrates how sentiment analysis is integrated into the RSS pipeline using Python and structured prompts. Rather than requesting a simple positive/negative output, we craft more complex and complete prompt demanding granular breakdowns, including

- Overall tone

- Primary emotion

- Emotional intensity

- Positive, negative, neutral, and informative elements

- Emotional impacts

This structured breakdown transforms sentiment from a single label into an intelligence profile.

By providing real-world examples—one English-language cybersecurity article and one German-language security article translated into English—you can see this method will work on a variety of languages.

These examples demonstrate that

- Sentiment analysis works across languages after normalization and translation

- The model can distinguish cautionary reporting from alarmist rhetoric

- Emotional intensity scoring provides prioritization context

This chapter addresses limitations, including sarcasm detection challenges, cultural interpretation risks, translation bias, and potential blending of reporting with opinion. This enhances the credibility of the analytical framework.

Threat Analysis As Operational Intelligence

The second half of the chapter shifts from tone measurement to risk evaluation. Threat analysis is clearly distinguished from sentiment analysis. While sentiment measures emotional polarity, threat analysis measures operational consequence. This distinction is critical and one of the strongest intellectual contributions of the chapter.

Threat analysis is defined as evaluation of content for indications of

- Cyber threats

- Physical threats

- Political instability

- Infrastructure risk

- Economic disruption

- Coordinated influence operations

- Emerging vulnerabilities

The chapter emphasizes that negative sentiment does not equal threat. A calmly written vulnerability report may represent high operational risk, while emotionally charged rhetoric may represent little actionable danger.

The chapter demonstrates how AI is directed, through carefully constructed prompts, to evaluate structured threat categories:

- Overall, Threat Level

- Threat Type

- Urgency

- Decision (ESCALATE/MONITOR/IGNORE)

- Confidence

- Rationale

This structure aligns closely with intelligence community reporting formats and provides machine-readable outputs suitable for dashboards and automated alerting.

Again, the chapter reinforces the methodology with two applied examples using the same articles analyzed in the sentiment section. These examples demonstrate

- An AI-enabled cyberattack trend report classified as Threat Level 4, Near-Term urgency, ESCALATE

- A government breach involving AI chatbots classified as Threat Level 4, Immediate urgency, ESCALATE

The threat rationale sections illustrate deep contextual reasoning, including geopolitical dimensions, infrastructure impact, and adversarial innovation patterns. This reinforces that the system is not merely detecting keywords but evaluating operational significance.

Integrating Sentiment and Threat

One of the strongest contributions of the chapter is the structured comparison between sentiment and threat:

- *Sentiment* measures tone; *threat* measures risk.

- *Sentiment* provides trend analysis; *threat* provides escalation decisions.

- *Sentiment* is often subjective; *threat* is action oriented.

The chapter culminates in a powerful conceptual insight:

Tone is the whisper. Threat is the warning. When combined, sentiment and threat analysis allow analysts to anticipate not only what is happening, but what may happen next. This layered model transforms RSS feeds into intelligence sensors capable of supporting predictive posture rather than reactive reporting.

Overall Impact of Chapter 6

This chapter elevates the book from technical RSS processing into applied intelligence methodology. It accomplishes several key advances:

1. It introduces structured AI reasoning into OSINT workflows.

2. It differentiates emotional analysis from operational threat evaluation.

3. It provides repeatable Python-based implementation patterns.

4. It demonstrates multilingual capability.

5. It establishes an escalation framework suitable for real-world security operations.

6. It bridges algorithmic processing and analyst-informed intelligence.

What to Expect in Chapter 7

Throughout this chapter, we enhanced our RSS intelligence pipeline with structured sentiment and threat analysis. Our system now classifies tone, evaluates risk, assigns threat levels, and supports escalation decisions. It prioritizes information rather than merely collecting it.

But there is still an important limit to consider. Every evaluation we have performed so far has been procedural. We defined the workflow. We instructed the model precisely what to assess. We determined the order of operations. In short, the system executed our logic and our detailed prompts.

What if the system could operate from a defined ***objective*** rather than a rigid sequence of steps?

What if, instead of telling the model *how* to process every feed, we defined the mission and allowed the system to decide which feeds require deeper analysis, which require escalation, and which can be ignored?

This is the transition from algorithmic processing to agentic intelligence.

Agentic AI systems operate with goals. They evaluate context, determine next steps, refine decisions, and iterate autonomously within defined boundaries. Rather than simply answering a prompt, an agent can

- Process multiple RSS feeds simultaneously

- Identify anomalies across feeds

- Re-prioritize attention dynamically

- Re-evaluate earlier decisions as new data emerges

- Escalate only when objective thresholds are met

In an OSINT environment, this capability is transformative. Instead of sequentially processing feeds one article at a time, an agentic system can monitor the entire ecosystem, reason across sources, and act according to mission-driven objectives.

In the next chapter, we will design and implement an Agentic AI framework that processes multiple RSS feeds, applies structured intelligence evaluation, and determines its own next analytical steps based on defined objectives. You will see how to move beyond scripted automation and into goal-directed intelligence orchestration using Python and AI.

This is where your RSS pipeline evolves from an intelligent tool into an autonomous analytical system.

## CHAPTER 7

Agentic AI for Multi-Feed Intelligence Processing

Until now, our RSS intelligence system has operated as a highly capable analytical engine. It retrieves feeds, normalizes content, translates multilingual sources, extracts entities, evaluates sentiment, and assigns structured threat scores. Each step has been deliberate, precise, and carefully defined.

Intelligence work is rarely linear. In real-world OSINT environments, analysts do not process information in rigid sequence because proactive research and analysis is always underway in anticipation of events rather than merely in response to events. Intel analysts shift focus when patterns emerge. They revisit earlier conclusions as new data appears. They prioritize anomalies. They escalate when risk intensifies. They ignore noise. In short, they operate utilizing ever-shifting objectives.

This chapter introduces a fundamental shift in how I apply AI to RSS intelligence processing: the transition from algorithmic workflows to agentic systems.

An algorithm follows instructions; an agent pursues a mission. Agentic AI allows us to define an objective such as identifying emerging cyber threats across multiple RSS feeds and empower the system to determine

C. Hosmer, *Extracting Intelligence from RSS News Feeds Using Python and AI*,
https://doi.org/10.1007/979-8-8688-2773-0_7

how best to achieve that goal. Rather than processing feeds one at a time in a predetermined order, the agent evaluates context, decides which feeds require deeper inspection, loops back when necessary, and escalates findings dynamically.

When applied to multi-feed OSINT monitoring, this capability transforms our pipeline from a structured processor into an autonomous intelligence assistant.

In this chapter, you will design and implement an agentic AI framework using Python and OpenAI that

1.   Monitors multiple RSS feeds simultaneously

2.   Utilizes contextual reasoning across sources

3.   Evaluates a set of RSS feeds simultaneously

4.   Delivers escalation decisions

5.   Operates according to mission-driven objectives

This is where automation evolves and your RSS intelligence system begins to think in terms of goals rather than individual steps. Once escalation identifies articles that need deeper analysis, I leverage our previous work to extract key details from each escalated article including Author profiling, Name Entity Recognition, and Sentiment/Threat Analysis.

What Is Agentic AI and How Does It Differ from Prompt-Driven Analysis

Up to this point in the book, I have primarily used Large Language Models (LLMs) in a *prompt-driven* manner. I provided carefully engineered instructions, supplied content from RSS feeds, and requested structured outputs such as summaries, named entities, sentiment scores, and threat assessments. The model responded and stopped. Each interaction was discreet, controlled, and bound by the specific instructions I provided.

Agentic AI represents a fundamental shift. Rather than simply responding to a single prompt, an agentic system is given an **objective** and autonomy to determine how best to achieve that objective. It can decide what steps to take, what tools to call, what information to retrieve, and when to loop back and reassess its findings. In short, prompt-driven AI answers questions. Agentic AI pursues goals.

Prompt-Driven Analysis: Structured but Reactive

In a prompt-driven workflow:

1. The OSINT developer defines the task.

2. The model executes exactly that task.

3. The process ends after the response.

For example:

- "Extract named entities from this article."

- "Translate this title into English."

- "Assess the threat level of this content."

Each prompt is explicit. Each response is final. The model does not determine what should happen next, the OSINT developer does.

This approach is powerful, precise, and predictable. It works exceptionally well when

- The workflow is linear.

- The rules are clearly defined.

- The sequence of operations is predetermined.

- You want tight control over every analytical step.

Much of our RSS processing pipeline so far has followed this pattern:

parse feed → clean text → translate → extract entities → assess sentiment → score threat.

That pipeline is in fact intelligent, but it is still procedural.

Agentic AI introduces three major conceptual differences:

Objective-Based Operation

Instead of issuing a task, you define an outcome using an objective.

What is an objective? Here is an example:

> *"Monitor multiple RSS feeds and escalate only credible, high-risk cybersecurity threats affecting U.S. critical infrastructure."*

The agent determines

- Which feeds to prioritize

- Which articles require deeper inspection

- When additional enrichment is needed

- Whether to escalate or dismiss content

- When to stop processing

You are no longer specifying *every step*. You are specifying the mission.

Iterative Reasoning and Self-Correction

Agentic systems can

- Loop over data

- Re-evaluate findings

- Call additional tools

- Adjust decisions based on intermediate results

A prompt-driven call is a single transaction. An agentic workflow is a reasoning cycle. This is what makes it powerful for OSINT.

In the real world, intelligence gathering is rarely linear.
Analysts:

- Revisit sources

- Cross-reference entities

- Re-score risk

- Seek corroboration

Agentic AI mirrors this investigative behavior.

Tool Awareness and Dynamic Execution

Traditional prompt calls treat the model as a text processor.
Agentic systems treat the model as a decision engine that can

- Call Python functions

- Retrieve external data

- Query additional RSS feeds

- Perform enrichment lookups

- Trigger alerts

The difference is subtle but profound: A loop in Python executes predefined logic. An agent determines what logic should be executed next. This is the moment when control shifts from rigid scripting to adaptive intelligence.

Why Agentic AI Matters for RSS-Driven OSINT

In an OSINT environment, especially when processing multiple RSS feeds:

- Volume is high.

- Signal-to-noise ratio is low.

- Threat relevance is contextual.

- Escalation criteria may evolve.

A prompt-driven system can analyze content.
An agentic system can manage intelligence flow.
It can

- Prioritize feeds dynamically

- Identify patterns across articles

- Correlate entities across sources

- Escalate only when confidence thresholds are met

- Avoid analyst fatigue

For cybersecurity monitoring, critical infrastructure protection, and real-time threat awareness, this shift from reactive analysis to autonomous decision support is transformative.

The Strategic Shift

Prompt-driven AI enhances workflows.

Agentic AI augments decision-making.

Prompt-driven AI is an intelligent tool.

Agentic AI begins to resemble a junior analyst.

In the next section, I will demonstrate how to apply this model to real-world RSS processing moving from scripted analysis to objective-driven autonomous intelligence.

Script 7-1 Agentic AI

For this example, I will

1) Provide a list of RSS feeds to analyze

2) Specify the number of recent articles to examine from each feed

3) Provide a clear Objective Statement to direct the agent

4) A Decision that classifies each article as one of the following:

   a) IGNORE—not relevant

   b) MONITOR—useful but not urgent

   c) ESCALATE—high-signal threat intelligence

5) Produce a PrettyTable result that includes the Decision, Reason for the Decision, Threat Level, Article Title, and the source RSS Feed. I then will save that result in a comma-separated value (CSV) file and a JavaScript Object Notation (JSON) file ready for processing by other intelligent systems.

Script Objective Statement

Here is our first Agentic AI Objective Statement in Python. I have kept this first example simple and straightforward, allowing the Agent to deliver the results.

```
OBJECTIVE = """
Identify articles that suggest emerging cyber threats,
active exploitation, nation-state activity,
critical infrastructure risk, or coordinated attacks.

Classify each article as:

IGNORE - not relevant
MONITOR - useful but not urgent
ESCALATE - high-signal threat intelligence

Return:
Decision:
Threat_Level: (1-5)
Reason: one sentence
"""
```

For this example, I have selected just three RSS feeds to be processed, and our script will process the most recent five articles from each feed. Here is the Python list of RSS feeds that will be processed:

```
RSS_FEED_LIST = ["https://www.cisa.gov/cybersecurity-advisories/all.xml",
                 "https://industrialcyber.co/feed/","https://www.infosecurity-magazine.com/rss/news/",
                 "https://krebsonsecurity.com/feed/"]
```

Examining the Main Loop

Next, I can examine the main loop of the script. As you can see, the main loop processes each RSS feed by obtaining the most recent five articles from each feed. For each article, the script calls the evaluate_article function that utilizes the OBJECTIVE that I have defined, passes the article title and summary to the function. Once each article is processed, I parse the raw AI output and extract the **Decision, Threat Level**, and **Reason** as define in the OBJECTIVE. Then I place the results in a PrettyTable and save the results in both a CSV JSON file. Below you will see the complete Python code for main, evaluate_article, and parseAgentOutput functions.

```python
if __name__ == "__main__":

    for eachFeed in RSS_FEED_LIST:
        feed = feedparser.parse(eachFeed)

        for entry in feed.entries[:5]:   # LIMIT investigation 5 most recent articles
            raw = evaluate_article(entry.title, entry.summary)
            parsed = parseAgentOutput(raw)

            decision = parsed.get("Decision")
            threat_level = int(parsed.get("Threat_Level"))
            reason = parsed.get("Reason")

            tbl.add_row([decision, reason, entry.title, eachFeed])

    tbl.sortby = "DECISION"

    print(tbl.get_string())

    csvPath = "Agentic-AI-Analysis-February-28-2026.csv"
    csv = tbl.get_csv_string()
    json = tbl.get_json_string()

    jsonPath = "Agentic-AI-Analysis-February-28-2026.json"

    with open(csvPath, "w", encoding="utf-8") as f:  # <-- key part
        f.write(csv)

    with open(jsonPath, "w", encoding="utf-8") as f:  # <-- key part
        f.write(json)
```

Top of Form

```python
def evaluate_article(title, summary):

    prompt = f"""
You are an autonomous OSINT threat detection agent.

OBJECTIVE:
{OBJECTIVE}

ARTICLE:
Title: {title}
Summary: {summary}
"""

    response = client.responses.create(
        model="gpt-5",
        input=prompt
    )

    return response.output_text
```

Bottom of Form

```python
def parseAgentOutput(text):

    lines = text.strip().split("\n")

    result = {}

    for line in lines:
        if ":" in line:
            key, value = line.split(":", 1)
            result[key.strip()] = value.strip()

    return result
```

Examining the Results

CSV excerpt viewed in Microsoft Excel.

DECISION	REASON	ARTICLE-TITLE	RSS-FEED
ESCALATE	A large IoT botnet (Kimwolf) is actively shifting C2 to I2P, disrupting the network and increasing resilience against takedown, indicating ongoing operations that may evade detection and impact enterprise-connected IoT devices.	Kimwolf Botnet Swamps Anonymity Network I2P	https://krebsonsecurity.com/feed/
ESCALATE	Active mobile espionage campaign using a trojanized Red Alert warning app distributed via SMS amid the Israelâ€'Iran conflict suggests likely nation-state	Israel: RedAlert Spyware Campaign Exploits Wartime Panic With Trojanized App	https://www.infosecurity-magazine.com/rss/news/
ESCALATE	CISA advisory reports critical unauthenticated OCPP/WebSocket vulnerabilities across all ePower EV charging stations enabling remote control and DoS of energy/transport infrastructure worldwide with no vendor fix, creating high	ePower epower.ie	https://www.cisa.gov/cybersecurity-advisories/all.xml
ESCALATE	Identifies an active operator coordinating attacks with the worldâ€™s largest DDoS botnet and provides attribution details, indicating immediate, high-impact threat	Who is the Kimwolf Botmaster â€œDortâ€?	https://krebsonsecurity.com/feed/
ESCALATE	New phishing-as-a-service â€œStarkillerâ€ enables adversary-in-the-middle proxying of real login pages to steal credentials and MFA codes, lowering the barrier to MFA-bypass attacks and likely driving rapid, hard-to-detect exploitation.	â€˜Starkillerâ€™ Phishing Service Proxies Real Login Pages, MFA	https://krebsonsecurity.com/feed/
ESCALATE	Reported surge in SloppyLemming espionage targeting defense, telecom, energy, and finance sectors in Pakistan and Bangladesh indicates likely nation-state activity with critical infrastructure risk and active targeting.	SloppyLemming espionage surge hitting defense, telecom, energy and finance in Pakistan and Bangladesh	https://industrialcyber.co/feed/
ESCALATE	Six Microsoft zero-days are being actively exploited in the wild, creating immediate risk to widely deployed Windows systems and requiring urgent patching.	Patch Tuesday, February 2026 Edition	https://krebsonsecurity.com/feed/
IGNORE	Article focuses on CISO workload and burnout, not on active threats, exploitation, or coordinated/nation-state activity.	Half of US CISOs Work the Equivalent of a Six-Day Week	https://www.infosecurity-magazine.com/rss/news/
IGNORE	Corporate spin-off branding news with no indicators of cyber threats, exploitation activity, or infrastructure risk.	Octave promises clarity and accountability as Hexagon spin-off takes shape	https://industrialcyber.co/feed/

JSON excerpt results.

```
  {
      "DECISION",
      "REASON",
      "ARTICLE-TITLE",
      "RSS-FEED"
  },
  {

      "ARTICLE-TITLE": "Kimwolf Botnet Swamps Anonymity Network I2P",
      "DECISION": "ESCALATE",
      "REASON": "A large IoT botnet (Kimwolf) is actively shifting C2 to I2P, disrupting the network and increasing resilience against
      takedown, indicating ongoing operations that may evade detection and impact enterprise-connected IoT devices.",
      "RSS-FEED": "https://krebsonsecurity.com/feed/"
  },
  {

      "ARTICLE-TITLE": "Israel: RedAlert Spyware Campaign Exploits Wartime Panic With Trojanized App",
      "DECISION": "ESCALATE",
      "REASON": "Active mobile espionage campaign using a trojanized Red Alert warning app distributed via SMS amid the Israel\u2013Iran
      conflict suggests likely nation-state activity and immediate risk to targeted users.",
      "RSS-FEED": "https://www.infosecurity-magazine.com/rss/news/"
  },
  {

      "ARTICLE-TITLE": "ePower epower.ie",
      "DECISION": "ESCALATE",
      "REASON": "CISA advisory reports critical unauthenticated OCPP/WebSocket vulnerabilities across all ePower EV charging stations
      enabling remote control and DoS of energy/transport infrastructure worldwide with no vendor fix, creating high immediate risk
      despite no confirmed exploitation.",
      "RSS-FEED": "https://www.cisa.gov/cybersecurity-advisories/all.xml"
  },
  {

      "ARTICLE-TITLE": "Who is the Kimwolf Botmaster \u201cDort\u201d?",
      "DECISION": "ESCALATE",
      "REASON": "Identifies an active operator coordinating attacks with the world\u2019s largest DDoS botnet and provides attribution
      details, indicating immediate, high-impact threat potential and coordinated activity.",
      "RSS-FEED": "https://krebsonsecurity.com/feed/"
  },
```

Script 7-2 Agentic AI Enhanced

Moving beyond the simple Agentic AI Objective Statement, the question is: "Can I enhance and have the Agentic engine do even more?" The enhanced Objective statement in Python is below. In this example, I direct the Objective Statement to dig deeper and generate an Author Profile along with all Name Entity Recognition (NER) that exists within the article (highlighted below). I then expanded the PrettyTable to include those results, so they appear in both the CSV and JSON results.

```python
OBJECTIVE = """
Identify articles that suggest threats to Industrial Control
or Critical Infrastructures, that could impact operations.

Classify each article as:

IGNORE - not relevant
MONITOR - useful but not urgent
ESCALATE - high-signal threat intelligence
Author_Profile
NER Name_Entity_Recognition

Return:
Decision:
Threat_Level: (1-5)
Author_Profile:
NER: create a python list
Reason: one sentence

"""
```

Main Loop 7-2

The main loop is expanded to accommodate and include the Author Profile and Name Entity Recognition for each article. In addition, instead of simply providing the article summary to the Agentic AI system, I extract the entire article from the article URL. This provides the Agentic AI system with more details to process. This context is important when performing intelligence analysis. This additional Python code also enhances the PrettyTable output for both the CSV and JSON results.

```python
if __name__ == "__main__":
    for eachFeed in RSS_FEED_LIST:
        feed = feedparser.parse(eachFeed)
        for entry in feed.entries[:5]:    # LIMIT investigation 5 most recent articles
            title  = entry.title
            try:
                author = entry.author
            except:
                author = "Unknown"
            url    = entry.link
            # download and parse the article
            article = Article(url)
            article.download()
            article.parse()
            # Obtain the article text
            articleText = article.text
            raw = evaluate_article(title, author, articleText)
            parsed = parseAgentOutput(raw)
            decision = parsed.get("Decision")
            threat_level = int(parsed.get("Threat_Level"))
            reason = parsed.get("Reason")
            try:
                authorProfile = parsed.get("Author_Profile")
            except:
                authorProfile = "NA"
            try:
                ner = parsed.get("NER")
                entities = ast.literal_eval(ner)
                cell = "\n".join(f"- {e}" for e in sorted(set(entities)))
            except:
                ner = "Unknown"
            tbl.add_row([decision, reason, entry.title, authorProfile, cell, eachFeed])
    tbl.sortby = "DECISION"
    csvPath = "Agentic-AI-Analysis-March-4-2026.csv"
    csv = tbl.get_csv_string()
    json = tbl.get_json_string()
    jsonPath = "Agentic-AI-Analysis-March-4-2026.json"
    with open(csvPath, "w", encoding="utf-8") as f:  # <-- key part
        f.write(csv)
    with open(jsonPath, "w", encoding="utf-8") as f:  # <-- key part
        f.write(json)
```

Examining the Results from Script 7-2

CSV excerpt viewed in Microsoft Excel.

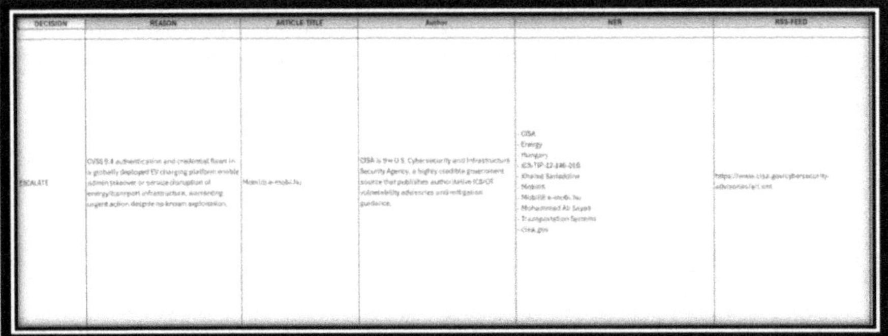

JSON except results.

```json
[
    [
        "DECISION",
        "REASON",
        "ARTICLE-TITLE",
        "Author",
        "NER",
        "RSS-FEED"
    ],
    {
        "ARTICLE-TITLE": "Mobiliti e-mobi.hu",
        "Author": "CISA (Cybersecurity and Infrastructure Security Agency, U.S. DHS) \u2013 authoritative ICS/OT advisories publisher with high credibility and direct visibility into critical infrastructure risks.",
        "DECISION": "ESCALATE",
        "NER": "- Mobiliti\n- Mobiliti e-mobi.hu\n- e-mobi.hu\n- CISA\n- Energy sector\n- Transportation Systems sector\n- Hungary\n- Worldwide\n- Khaled Sarieddine\n- Mohammad Ali Sayed\n- CVSS v3 9.4\n- ICS\n- ICS-TIP-12-146-01B\n- 2026-03-03",
        "REASON": "Critical EV charging platform vulnerabilities (missing auth, weak sessions/credentials) enable admin takeover or DoS of charging infrastructure across energy/transport sectors, demanding urgent triage despite no known exploitation.",
        "RSS-FEED": "https://www.cisa.gov/cybersecurity-advisories/all.xml"
    },
    {
        "ARTICLE-TITLE": "Hitachi Energy RTU500 Product",
        "Author": "CISA (U.S. Cybersecurity and Infrastructure Security Agency) republishing Hitachi Energy PSIRT CSAF advisory; authoritative ICS/OT vulnerability notice with mitigation guidance (republished 2026-03-03).",
        "DECISION": "MONITOR",
        "NER": "- CISA\n- Cybersecurity and Infrastructure Security Agency\n- Hitachi Energy\n- RTU500\n- RTU500 series CMU Firmware\n- Critical Manufacturing\n- Switzerland\n- CSAF\n- CVSS v3 7.5\n- Improper Handling of Insufficient Permissions or Privileges\n- Incomplete List of Disallowed Inputs\n- Uncontrolled Recursion\n- Allocation of Resources Without Limits or Throttling\n- PSIRT\n- 8DBD000237\n- ICS-TIP-12-146-01B\n- VPN",
        "REASON": "CVSS 7.5 vulnerabilities in Hitachi Energy RTU500 can lead to device outages impacting ICS operations, but no active exploitation is noted, warranting prioritized monitoring and remediation rather than immediate escalation.",
        "RSS-FEED": "https://www.cisa.gov/cybersecurity-advisories/all.xml"
    }
]
```

Summary

This chapter marks a significant evolution in the design of our RSS intelligence system. In previous chapters, we built a powerful analytical pipeline capable of retrieving feeds, translating multilingual content, extracting named entities, profiling authors, and evaluating sentiment and threat levels. While highly effective, that system remained fundamentally procedural. Each step was defined in advance and executed in a strict sequence determined by the developer.

This chapter introduces a transformative concept: **Agentic AI**.

Agentic systems move beyond traditional prompt-driven interactions by operating according to **objectives rather than instructions**. Instead of telling the model exactly what task to perform at each stage, I define the mission and allow the system to determine how best to achieve that outcome. In practical terms, this shifts our RSS processing framework from a rigid workflow into a **goal-oriented intelligence assistant capable of reasoning, prioritizing, and escalating findings dynamically**.

Through the development of two Python-based implementations, this chapter demonstrates how an agentic architecture can monitor multiple RSS feeds simultaneously, evaluate articles in context, and determine whether information should be ignored, monitored, or escalated as potential threat intelligence. The agent analyzes content, assigns threat levels, explains its reasoning, and produces structured outputs that can be consumed by downstream analytical systems.

The enhanced implementation further expands the agent's capabilities by incorporating **full-article analysis, author profiling, and named entity recognition**, enabling deeper contextual understanding and richer intelligence outputs. The results are presented in structured formats using PrettyTable and exported to both **CSV and JSON**, making the intelligence easily accessible for reporting, visualization, and integration with other security tools.

More importantly, this chapter highlights the conceptual shift required to design effective agentic systems. Prompt-driven AI remains a powerful tool for precise analytical tasks, but Agentic AI introduces autonomy, iterative reasoning, and tool awareness capabilities that closely resemble the investigative behavior of human analysts. In environments such as cybersecurity monitoring and OSINT analysis, where signals must be separated from overwhelming volumes of noise, this approach dramatically improves scalability and responsiveness.

By the end of this chapter, you have transformed your RSS intelligence pipeline into an **objective-driven intelligence system capable of adaptive analysis across multiple information sources**. This capability represents a critical step toward building AI systems that not only process information but actively support investigative decision-making.

Chapter Challenge: Enhancing the Agent's Objective

Throughout this chapter, we demonstrated how an agentic AI system can process RSS feeds by working toward a clearly defined **objective statement** rather than responding to a single prompt. In our examples, the agent evaluated RSS articles and determined whether the content represented a meaningful cybersecurity threat that should be escalated.

However, the objective statement we used was intentionally simple so the mechanics of the agent could be clearly understood.

Real-world intelligence systems rarely operate with such narrow objectives. Analysts often refine mission statements to include additional context, priorities, and operational constraints. One of the most powerful ways to improve an agentic system is to enhance the **objective itself**.

Your challenge is to redesign the objective statement used by the agent in this chapter.

Consider how the agent might behave differently if the objective included additional requirements such as

- **Geographic Prioritization**

  - Escalate threats that impact specific regions or countries.

- **Critical Infrastructure Focus**

  - Prioritize threats affecting sectors such as energy, transportation, healthcare, or communications.

- **Source Credibility Weighting**

  - Increase confidence for information originating from government advisories, security vendors, or well-established news organizations.

- **Cross-Source Corroboration**

  - Require confirmation of an event across multiple independent sources before escalation.

- **Recent Event Relevance**

  - Escalate only emerging or recently discovered threats rather than historical reporting.

- **Entity Enrichment**

  - Investigate organizations, vulnerabilities, threat actors, or technologies mentioned in the article before making a final decision.

You may find that modifying the objective statement alone can dramatically change the behavior of the agent without altering the underlying Python code.

Suggested Exercise

Modify the objective statement used in this chapter to create an agent that

1. Focuses specifically on **Operational Technology (OT) and Industrial Control Systems (ICS)** threats

2. Prioritizes articles referencing **known exploited vulnerabilities**

3. Escalates events that affect **critical infrastructure sectors**

Run your agent against several RSS feeds and observe how the agent's decisions change.

Next Steps

In Chapter 8, I will apply our Agentic AI Script (with some tweaks) to a series of real-world case studies spanning multiple domains (you should do the same). These examples will demonstrate how the integration of Python and artificial intelligence can transform raw RSS feeds into actionable intelligence. By combining automated data collection, contextual analysis, and objective-driven AI reasoning, I will show how modern analytical pipelines can identify emerging patterns, surface meaningful insights, and deliver measurable impact in environments where timely information matters most.

## CHAPTER 8

Real-World Applications and Case Studies

Up to this point in our journey, we have focused primarily on cybersecurity as the proving ground for applying Python and AI to RSS-based OSINT analysis. Along the way, we developed the tools, methods, and architectural patterns necessary to transform raw information streams into meaningful intelligence. We built scripts capable of retrieving feeds, cleaning and normalizing content, extracting entities, analyzing sentiment and relevance, and ultimately deployed an **Agentic AI workflow** capable of making analytical decisions.

Now it's time to expand the horizon.

The techniques you have learned in the previous chapters are not limited to cybersecurity. In fact, one of the most exciting aspects of combining Python with Agentic AI is that the same analytical framework can be applied to **virtually any domain where information is flowing in real time**.

RSS feeds provide a continuous stream of observations from scientists, journalists, researchers, and institutions around the world. When paired with AI-driven analysis, those streams can become powerful sources of insight.

© Chet Hosmer 2026

C. Hosmer, *Extracting Intelligence from RSS News Feeds Using Python and AI*,
https://doi.org/10.1007/979-8-8688-2773-0_8

In this chapter, we will step beyond cybersecurity and explore how Agentic AI can be applied to a variety of fascinating real-world domains. Together we will examine how the same framework can be used to monitor developments in **space exploration** and the **climate change** debate. Each case study demonstrates how a simple change in the agent's objective and information sources allows the system to adapt to an entirely new analytical mission.

Think of the Agentic AI framework you have built as a kind of **intelligence engine**. By changing the objective statement and selecting new sources of information, the engine can pivot from detecting cybersecurity threats to identifying newly discovered celestial objects, monitoring global political developments, or highlighting emerging scientific breakthroughs.

In the sections that follow, we will walk through two practical case studies that illustrate how this approach works in practice. Along the way, you will see how small changes in agent objectives and feed selection can dramatically change the insights that emerge from the data. By the end of the chapter, you will not only understand how to apply Agentic AI across multiple domains you will also be equipped to design your own intelligent monitoring systems for virtually any topic that interests you.

So, buckle up. The tools are built, the agents are ready, and the data streams are flowing. It's time to put our system to work in the real world.

Space Exploration Agentic AI OSINT

One of my personal interests involves space exploration. Space exploration has entered a remarkable new era of discovery. Advances in telescope technology, robotic exploration, and international collaboration have dramatically increased the pace at which new astronomical observations are being made. From powerful observatories such as the James Webb Space Telescope to large-scale survey projects scanning the sky for transient objects, scientists are now able to observe the universe with unprecedented sensitivity and detail. As a result, discoveries that once took years to uncover can now emerge in rapid succession, often reported through scientific publications, institutional press releases, and astronomy-focused news sources.

One particularly fascinating area of research involves the detection and analysis of objects that may have originated outside our own solar system. The discovery of the interstellar visitor 'Oumuamua, followed by the comet 2I/Borisov, demonstrated that material from other star systems can occasionally pass through our cosmic neighborhood, 3I/ATLAS that has recently garnered significant scientific study and debate.

Each new detection provides valuable scientific insight into planetary formation processes beyond our solar system. Because these objects travel quickly and may only be observable for a limited period, rapid awareness of new discoveries and observational updates is essential for the astronomical community.

At the same time, astronomers around the world are continually identifying new comets, asteroids, and near-Earth objects through automated sky surveys and telescope networks. Organizations such as NASA's planetary defense programs and international observatories regularly publish updates describing new detections, orbital calculations, and follow-up observations. These developments often appear first in online news sources, institutional announcements, and science reporting, many of which provide RSS feeds that can be monitored programmatically. It is worth noting that as these fast-moving events become more widely known throughout the community, adding to the knowledge base, we also can use Agentic AI to help predict possible other events and narrow down some of the places to look in a very large area!

This environment makes space exploration an ideal domain for applying an Agentic AI-driven OSINT framework. By collecting and analyzing RSS feeds from astronomy news outlets, research institutions, and space agencies, an intelligent monitoring system can continuously scan for reports of newly discovered objects, unusual observations, or significant scientific findings. Instead of manually searching for updates across dozens of sources, the AI agent can evaluate each incoming article, extract relevant entities such as object names, observatories, and scientists, and determine whether the information warrants further attention.

In this case study, we will apply the Agentic AI framework developed in earlier chapters to monitor space-related information sources and identify articles describing astronomical discoveries and observational science. By defining a specialized objective and selecting RSS feeds related to astronomy and space research, the agent becomes capable of detecting reports about newly observed celestial objects, unusual phenomena, and significant developments in our understanding of the universe. This example demonstrates how the same approach used for cybersecurity monitoring can be adapted to explore one of humanity's most important frontiers, the ongoing exploration of space.

Script-Chapter-8-SpaceResearch.py

The first step of course is to develop an Agentic AI Objective statement that we can apply to this subject, here is the draft that is included in the **Chapter-8-SpaceResearch.py script.**

```
OBJECTIVE = """
Analyze RSS articles for developments related to interstellar objects,
candidate interstellar objects, comets, asteroids, near-Earth objects,
and unusual small-body discoveries in the solar system.

Give special attention to:
- newly discovered objects
- unusual orbital trajectories
- hyperbolic or high-velocity objects
- follow-up observations of newly detected bodies
- telescope observations from major observatories
- interstellar objects
- hyperbolic trajectories
- extrasolar origin of objects
- unusual comet or asteroid velocities
- high-velocity small bodies
- objects entering from outside the solar system
- scientific debate about Oumuamua or similar objects

Classify each article as:

IGNORE   - not related to astronomical object discovery or observation
MONITOR  - astronomy related and discusses objects or observations
ESCALATE - reports discovery, unusual behavior, or major analysis of a celestial object

Return:
Decision
Interstellar
Object_Name
Observation_Type
Author_Profile
Reason
"""
```

Now that we have an Agentic AI Objective, we need to research and define a few relevant RSS feeds to test with. Here is what we have come up with so far.

```
SPACE_FEEDS = ["https://www.nasa.gov/rss/dyn/breaking_news.rss",
               "https://www.space.com/feeds/all",
               "https://www.universetoday.com/feed/",
               "https://minorplanetcenter.net/rss.xml",
               "https://cneos.jpl.nasa.gov/rss.xml",
               "https://spaceweather.com/rss.xml",
               "https://www.sciencedaily.com/rss/space_time/astronomy.xml"
               "https://phys.org/rss-feed/space-news/"
]
```

I encourage you to modify and enhance the Objective and related RSS feeds as you experiment with this script. Let's examine an excerpt from the results: The results properly identified several relevant articles.

DECISION	INTERSTELLER	REASON	OBJECT-NAME	OBSERVATION-TYPE	ARTICLE-TITLE	AUTHOR	RSS-FEED
ESCALATE	Yes	Confirms water release from an interstellar comet with unexpectedly strong activity far from the Sun; third confirmed interstellar comet; significant follow-up using a major NASA observatory with peer-reviewed results.	3I/ATLAS	Space-based ultraviolet observations (NASA Swift/UVOT) detecting OH emission indicating water outgassing (~40 kg/s) at ~3 AU	Interstellar comet 3I/ATLAS is spraying water across the solar system	Unknown; quotes Auburn University team (Dennis Bodewits, Zexi Xing, April lead author)	https://www.sciencedaily.com/rss/space_time/astronomy.xml
ESCALATE	Yes	Major telescope study of an interstellar comet reports unusually high methanol-to-HCN ratios (19‰ '70â€"120) and distinct outgassing sources (HCN from nucleus; CH3OH from nucleus and icy grains), indicating atypical formation conditions versus solar system comets and providing key chemical/physical constraints on an extrasolar small body.	3I/ATLAS	ALMA (Atacama Compact Array) submillimeter spectroscopy and spatial mapping of coma species (CH3OH, HCN; abundance ratios and outgassing behavior analysis	An interstellar comet packed with alcohol? What ALMA found in 3I/ATLAS	Lead author Nathan X. Roth (American University); study posted on arXiv (2025) analyzing ALMA ACA data	https://phys.org/rss-feed/space-news/
ESCALATE	No	Newly discovered NEO received high-precision follow-up with a major observatory (JWST), refining its trajectory and ruling out a lunar impact while predicting a very close pass; significant update on a potentially hazardous object's orbit.	2024 YR4	JWST follow-up astrometry and orbit refinement; impact risk assessment; predicted close lunar flyby (2032-12-22)	Good news for the moon: Famous asteroid 2024 YR4 won't smash into it in 2032	Keith Cooper, Space.com science journalist covering astronomy and space missions	https://www.space.com/feeds/all
ESCALATE	No	Peer-reviewed analysis directly detects a DART-induced change in the system's solar orbit (19‰ "0.15 s), the first measured human-made alteration of a celestial body's heliocentric trajectory. Based on 22 stellar occultations and long-term tracking, this is a major result for small-body dynamics and planetary defense, meriting elevated monitoring despite not being interstellar.	Didymosâ€"Dimorphos binary asteroid system	Post-impact follow-up via stellar occultations; heliocentric orbit change measurement; planetary defense validation	NASA's DART test for planetary defense proved it can shift an asteroid's solar orbit	AFP science report referencing peer-reviewed study by Rahil Makadia et al. (Science Advances, 2026) and NASA statements	https://phys.org/rss-feed/space-news/

The most promising are two recent ones directly related to 3I/ATLAS that provide new details regarding water and possibly alcohol detections. Interestingly, during testing the system frequently classified articles as MONITOR rather than ESCALATE. This reflects the rarity of true interstellar detections and highlights an important aspect of OSINT analysis: meaningful signals are often buried within large volumes of routine information.

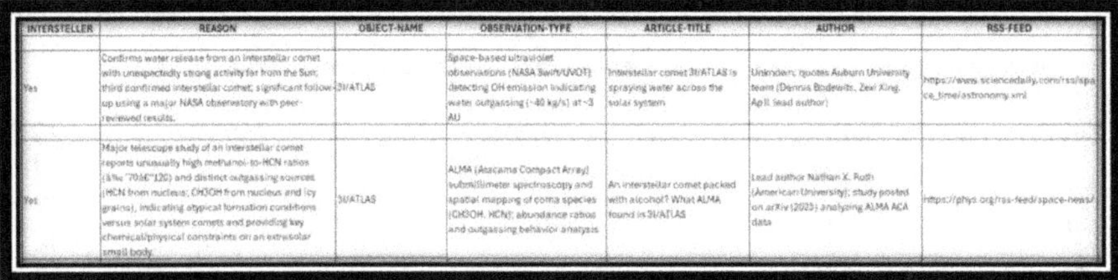

INTERSTELLER	REASON	OBJECT-NAME	OBSERVATION-TYPE	ARTICLE-TITLE	AUTHOR	RSS-FEED
Yes	Confirms water release from an interstellar comet with unexpectedly strong activity far from the Sun; third confirmed interstellar comet; significant follow-up using a major NASA observatory with peer-reviewed results.	3I/ATLAS	Space-based ultraviolet observations (NASA Swift/UVOT) detecting OH emission indicating water outgassing (~40 kg/s) at ~3 AU	Interstellar comet 3I/ATLAS is spraying water across the solar system	Unknown; quotes Auburn University team (Dennis Bodewits, Zexi Xing, April lead author)	https://www.sciencedaily.com/rss/space_time/astronomy.xml
Yes	Major telescope study of an interstellar comet reports unusually high methanol-to-HCN ratios (19‰ '70â€"120) and distinct outgassing sources (HCN from nucleus; CH3OH from nucleus and icy grains), indicating atypical formation conditions versus solar system comets and providing key chemical/physical constraints on an extrasolar small body.	3I/ATLAS	ALMA (Atacama Compact Array) submillimeter spectroscopy and spatial mapping of coma species (CH3OH, HCN; abundance ratios and outgassing behavior analysis	An interstellar comet packed with alcohol? What ALMA found in 3I/ATLAS	Lead author Nathan X. Roth (American University); study posted on arXiv (2025) analyzing ALMA ACA data	https://phys.org/rss-feed/space-news/

In addition, a non-interstellar yet important article surrounding 2024 YR4 that asserts it will not crash into the moon as previously feared was found.

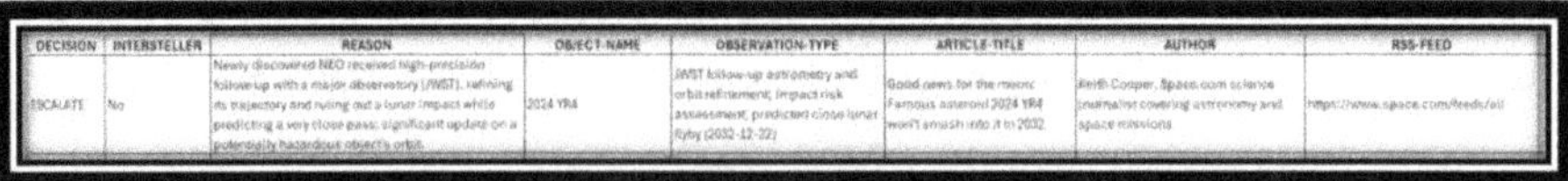

DECISION	INTERSTELLER	REASON	OBJECT-NAME	OBSERVATION-TYPE	ARTICLE-TITLE	AUTHOR	RSS-FEED
ESCALATE	No	Newly discovered NEO received high-precision follow-up with a major observatory (JWST), refining its trajectory and ruling out a lunar impact while predicting a very close pass; significant update on a potentially hazardous object's orbit.	2024 YR4	JWST follow-up astrometry and orbit refinement; impact risk assessment; predicted close lunar flyby (2032-12-22)	Good news for the moon: Famous asteroid 2024 YR4 won't smash into it in 2032	Keith Cooper, Space.com science journalist covering astronomy and space missions	https://www.space.com/feeds/all

Overall, the Agent returned over 150 articles that met our criteria. I encourage you to execute the script on your own either as is or with your own modifications of the Agentic AI Objective and by expanding the list of feeds to process.

Climate Change Agentic AI OSINT

The next study involves a highly debated topic relating to climate change. Few scientific topics today generate as much global attention and as much public debate as climate change. Over the past several decades, climate science has evolved into one of the most actively studied areas of research, involving thousands of scientists, international collaborations, and vast networks of observational instruments measuring changes in Earth's atmosphere, oceans, and ecosystems. At the same time, discussions surrounding climate change extend far beyond the scientific community, influencing geopolitical and military policy, economic strategy, energy development, and public perception around the world.

New research findings, government reports, environmental observations, and policy proposals are published almost daily. Organizations such as the National Oceanic and Atmospheric Administration (NOAA), the National Aeronautics and Space Administration (NASA), and the Intergovernmental Panel on Climate Change regularly release data and reports that contribute to the broader scientific understanding of climate trends. At the same time, policymakers, economists, and advocacy groups debate how best to respond to these findings. As a result, the public conversation around climate change is not limited to scientific discovery, it also includes discussions of environmental policy, economic impacts, technological innovation, and societal priorities.

Because the climate change discussion spans scientific, political, and social domains, it provides an excellent example of how OSINT techniques can be used to monitor complex and evolving narratives. Articles may report new scientific measurements, describe the impacts of extreme weather events, highlight technological developments in renewable energy, or discuss legislative and policy responses. Each of these perspectives contributes to a broader understanding of how climate-related issues are being interpreted and debated across different sectors of society.

In this case study, we will apply our Agentic AI framework to monitor RSS feeds containing climate and environmental reporting. By defining an objective focused on identifying climate-related research, policy developments, and debate-driven narratives, the AI agent can evaluate incoming articles and determine their relevance to the broader climate change discussion. Through this process, the system can help identify emerging themes, track evolving viewpoints, and highlight significant developments appearing across scientific publications, news outlets, and policy discussions.

This example demonstrates another powerful capability of the Python-based OSINT framework we have built throughout this book. By simply adjusting the agent's objective and selecting information sources focused on climate and environmental reporting, the same analytical system used for cybersecurity monitoring and space exploration can be repurposed to analyze one of the most important scientific and societal debates of our time.

The first step of course is to develop an Agentic AI Objective statement that can be applied to this subject. Here is the draft included in the **Chapter-8-Climate-Change.py script.**

```
OBJECTIVE = """
Analyze the RSS feed article for relevance to the global climate change discussion,
with particular attention to scientific findings, environmental observations,
policy developments, and societal debate regarding climate change.

The goal is to identify articles that provide meaningful insight into:
• new scientific research or climate measurements
• environmental observations related to climate trends
• policy decisions or governmental responses
• technological developments related to climate mitigation
• economic or social perspectives influencing the climate debate

Classify each article as:
IGNORE   - not related to climate change, environmental science, or the broader climate debate
MONITOR  - relevant to climate science, environmental trends, or ongoing policy discussions
ESCALATE - reports significant scientific findings, major policy actions, influential studies,
           or developments likely to impact public understanding or decision making

Return the results in the following format:
Decision:
Category:
Author_Profile:
Reason:

Field requirements:
Decision:
Must be IGNORE, MONITOR, or ESCALATE
Category:
Indicate the primary focus of the article. Use one of the following:
SCIENCE
POLICY
TECHNOLOGY
ECONOMICS
SOCIAL

Author_Profile:
Provide a short description of the author or organization if available

Reason:
Provide one concise sentence explaining the classification decision
"""
```

In addition to the Objective statement, we need a list of related RSS feeds. Here is our initial list. (Note: Feel free to expand this list as you experiment with the script.)

```
CLIMATE_FEEDS = ["https://climate.nasa.gov/news/rss.xml",
                "https://www.noaa.gov/news-release/rss.xml",
                "https://www.nature.com/subjects/climate-change/rss",
                "https://www.sciencedaily.com/rss/earth_climate/global_warming.xml",
                "https://yaleclimateconnections.org/feed/",
                "https://insideclimatenews.org/feed/",
                "https://www.carbonbrief.org/feed/",
                "https://www.technologyreview.com/topic/climate-change/feed/"
]
```

Monitoring the climate change discussion requires collecting information from a diverse set of sources. Scientific institutions publish new research findings, government agencies report environmental observations, policy organizations discuss regulatory responses, and technology publications highlight innovations intended to address climate challenges. By aggregating feeds from each of these areas, the Agentic AI system can observe climate discussion from multiple perspectives.

Here is an excerpt of the results generated by the Climate-Change script using the defined feeds and Agentic AI Objective.

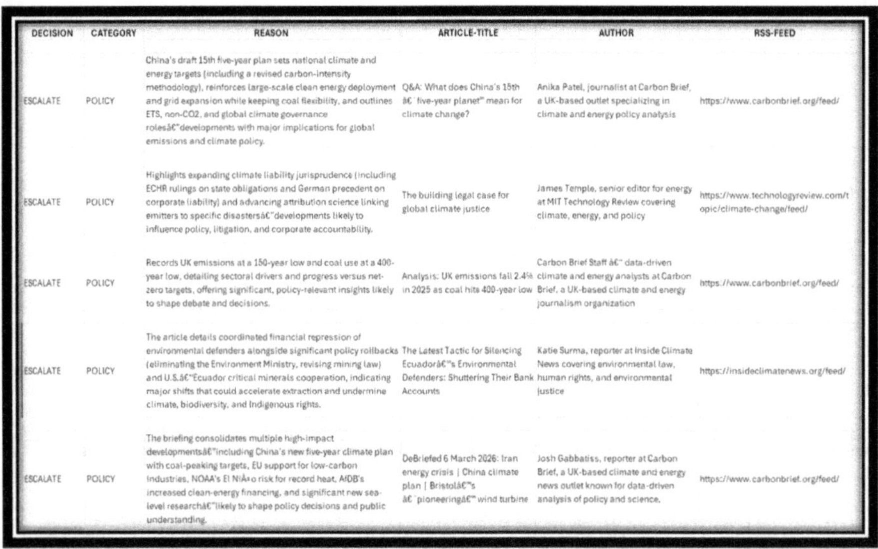

DECISION	CATEGORY	REASON	ARTICLE-TITLE	AUTHOR	RSS-FEED
ESCALATE	POLICY	China's draft 15th five-year plan sets national climate and energy targets (including a revised carbon-intensity methodology), reinforces large-scale clean energy deployment and grid expansion while keeping coal flexibility, and outlines ETS, non-CO2, and global climate governance rolesâ€"developments with major implications for global emissions and climate policy.	Q&A: What does China's 15th â€ five-year planet™ mean for climate change?	Anika Patel, journalist at Carbon Brief, a UK-based outlet specializing in climate and energy policy analysis	https://www.carbonbrief.org/feed/
ESCALATE	POLICY	Highlights expanding climate liability jurisprudence (including ECHR rulings on state obligations and German precedent on corporate liability) and advancing attribution science linking emitters to specific disastersâ€"developments likely to influence policy, litigation, and corporate accountability.	The building legal case for global climate justice	James Temple, senior editor for energy at MIT Technology Review covering climate, energy, and policy	https://www.technologyreview.com/topic/climate-change/feed/
ESCALATE	POLICY	Records UK emissions at a 150-year low and coal use at a 400-year low, detailing sectoral drivers and progress versus net-zero targets, offering significant, policy-relevant insights likely to shape debate and decisions.	Analysis: UK emissions fall 2.4% in 2025 as coal hits 400-year low	Carbon Brief Staff â€" data-driven climate and energy analysts at Carbon Brief, a UK-based climate and energy journalism organization	https://www.carbonbrief.org/feed/
ESCALATE	POLICY	The article details coordinated financial repression of environmental defenders alongside significant policy rollbacks (eliminating the Environment Ministry, revising mining law) and U.S.â€"Ecuador critical minerals cooperation, indicating major shifts that could accelerate extraction and undermine climate, biodiversity, and Indigenous rights.	The Latest Tactic for Silencing Ecuadorâ€™s Environmental Defenders: Shuttering Their Bank Accounts	Katie Surma, reporter at Inside Climate News covering environmental law, human rights, and environmental justice	https://insideclimatenews.org/feed/
ESCALATE	POLICY	The briefing consolidates multiple high-impact developmentsâ€"including China's new five-year climate plan with coal-peaking targets, EU support for low-carbon industries, NOAA's El Niño risk for record heat, AfDB's increased clean-energy financing, and significant new sea-level researchâ€"likely to shape policy decisions and public understanding.	DeBriefed 6 March 2026: Iran energy crisis	China climate plan	Bristolâ€™s â€ pioneeringâ€™ wind turbine	Josh Gabbatiss, reporter at Carbon Brief, a UK-based climate and energy news outlet known for data-driven analysis of policy and science.	https://www.carbonbrief.org/feed/

Summary

In this chapter, we moved beyond the cybersecurity-focused examples explored in earlier sections and demonstrated how the same Python-based OSINT framework can be applied to entirely different domains of inquiry. By combining RSS feed aggregation with Agentic AI analysis, we showed how a flexible intelligence pipeline can be adapted to monitor diverse information environments with only minor adjustments to the agent's objective and data sources.

The first case study explored **space exploration and astronomical discovery**, illustrating how the system can be used to monitor scientific observations, newly discovered celestial objects, and developments in observational astronomy. By defining an objective tailored to astronomical research and selecting RSS feeds from space agencies, observatories, and scientific publications, the agent was able to identify articles describing unusual objects, follow-up observations, and ongoing scientific debate surrounding interstellar visitors and near-Earth objects. This example demonstrated how AI-assisted OSINT techniques can help researchers quickly identify meaningful discoveries within a large stream of routine reporting.

The second case study focused on **climate change**, one of the most widely discussed scientific and policy topics of our time. Here the Agentic AI framework was used to monitor a broad spectrum of climate-related information sources, including scientific institutions, environmental reporting outlets, and policy-focused publications. By analyzing articles that reflect scientific research, policy developments, technological innovation, and societal perspectives, the agent was able to identify relevant developments and highlight emerging themes within the ongoing global discussion surrounding climate change.

Together, these case studies demonstrate a central insight of this book: once the underlying intelligence pipeline is established, the system becomes highly adaptable. By simply modifying the **Agentic AI objective and the set of monitored RSS feeds**, the same analytical framework can be repurposed to explore entirely new domains of knowledge. What began as a cybersecurity monitoring tool can quickly evolve into a broader OSINT platform capable of tracking scientific discoveries, geopolitical developments, environmental research, or technological innovation.

Ultimately, the real power of this approach lies in its flexibility. Python provides the automation and data-handling capabilities needed to collect and process large volumes of information, while Agentic AI supplies the analytical reasoning required to interpret that information in context. When combined, these technologies create a powerful and extensible system for transforming raw information streams into meaningful insight.

As you continue experimenting with the scripts presented in this chapter, consider how you might expand the system by further adding new domains, refining objectives, or integrating additional data sources. The possibilities are limited only by the questions you wish to explore and the information streams available to analyze.

Chapter 9: What Lies Ahead?

In Chapter 9, we will reach into our crystal ball and attempt to predict the future of Python and Agentic AI. The tools we have built throughout this book represent only the beginning of a much larger transformation in how intelligent systems gather and interpret information. In this final chapter, we will look ahead to emerging trends, new capabilities, and the exciting possibilities that lie just over the technological horizon.

Future Agentic AI RSS Feed Analysis

Throughout this book, we have built a complete pipeline for transforming raw RSS feeds into meaningful intelligence using Python and artificial intelligence. We began with the fundamentals of acquiring feeds and extracting content, then progressively enhanced our system by integrating OpenAI models for translation, entity extraction, sentiment analysis, threat evaluation, and finally an Agentic AI workflow capable of making structured decisions about the information it processes.

While the techniques demonstrated in this book are powerful today, they also represent only the beginning of what will soon be possible. The future of RSS intelligence systems will likely move beyond periodic analysis toward continuously operating intelligent agents that actively monitor, analyze, and prioritize information in near real time.

In this final chapter, we briefly explore where this technology is heading and how systems like the one we developed may evolve in the coming years.

© Chet Hosmer 2026
C. Hosmer, *Extracting Intelligence from RSS News Feeds Using Python and AI*,
https://doi.org/10.1007/979-8-8688-2773-0_9

From Static Analysis to Continuous Intelligence

In the examples presented throughout this book, our Python scripts retrieve RSS feeds and process them when the script is executed. This approach works extremely well for demonstrations, research, and structured analysis tasks. However, future implementations will likely move toward continuous intelligence systems that operate automatically in the background.

Rather than waiting for a user to initiate analysis, an intelligent monitoring system would constantly search for newly published articles within selected domains such as cybersecurity, space exploration, geopolitical developments, or any topic of interest.

In this model, the system becomes an always-running observer that continuously scans trusted information sources, identifies new articles as they appear, and prepares them for analysis.

The result is a shift from on-demand analysis to persistent awareness.

Autonomous Discovery of Relevant Information

Another natural evolution of the system described in this book is the ability for an Agentic AI framework to discover new content on its own and/or be able to infer new information/knowledge by consolidating numerous content sources, including content sources in other fields?

In earlier chapters, we defined a specific set of RSS feeds that the system would process. While curated feeds provide high-quality information, the next generation of systems may extend this capability by allowing the AI agent to actively search for additional relevant sources.

An intelligent agent could periodically

- Identify newly published articles within a defined topic area

- Discover additional RSS feeds or publications covering similar subjects

- Evaluate the credibility and relevance of these new sources

- Add high-value sources to its monitoring list

This capability would allow the intelligence pipeline to expand organically, improving its coverage of emerging developments without requiring manual updates.

Over time, the system would evolve from a static feed list into a dynamic ecosystem of trusted information sources.

Continuous Agentic Processing

Once new information has been discovered, the next logical step is to automatically apply the Agentic AI analysis framework introduced in Chapter 7.

In such a system, newly identified articles would immediately pass through the same analytical stages we developed earlier:

- Content extraction

- Language normalization and translation

- Entity recognition and enrichment

- Sentiment and threat analysis

- Agentic evaluation against a defined objective

Rather than analyzing historical data after the fact, the system would perform these steps immediately as new information appears. This enables near real-time interpretation of emerging developments across multiple domains.

Intelligent Alerting and Notification

Perhaps the most valuable capability of future Agentic systems will be their ability to notify analysts only when something important occurs.

One of the greatest challenges in open source intelligence is not the lack of information, but rather the overwhelming volume of available data. Analysts often struggle to determine which articles truly require attention.

Agentic AI systems can help solve this problem by acting as intelligent filters. After evaluating newly discovered articles, the system could automatically notify users when specific conditions are met, such as

- Detection of a high-severity cybersecurity threat

- Emerging geopolitical developments

- Significant scientific discoveries

- Indicators of coordinated activity across multiple sources

Instead of manually reviewing hundreds of articles, analysts would receive targeted notifications highlighting only the most important findings.

This dramatically improves signal-to-noise ratio while allowing analysts to focus on interpretation rather than data collection.

The Role of Human Oversight

Despite the increasing capabilities of AI-driven analysis systems, human expertise and control will remain essential.

Agentic AI systems can rapidly process large volumes of information, identify patterns, and flag anomalies. However, final interpretation, contextual understanding, and decision-making still require human judgment. The most effective systems will therefore combine: Machine scale with human insight.

In this partnership, AI performs the heavy lifting of data collection and preliminary analysis, while human analysts provide the strategic understanding necessary to interpret the results.

Python As the Foundation of Intelligent Analysis

One reason the techniques described in this book are so powerful is the role that Python plays in bringing all these components together.

Python continues to be one of the most important languages in artificial intelligence, data science, and cybersecurity research. Its extensive ecosystem of libraries allows developers to integrate

- RSS feed processing

- Natural language analysis

- Machine Learning Models

- AI services

- Data visualization and reporting

Because of this flexibility, Python will almost certainly remain a foundational tool for building intelligent information processing systems.

As AI capabilities continue to evolve, Python will remain the glue that allows researchers, analysts, and developers to rapidly integrate new technologies into practical workflows.

Final Thoughts

The system developed in this book demonstrates how Python and artificial intelligence can transform raw RSS feeds into actionable intelligence. By combining structured data collection with AI-driven analysis and Agentic decision frameworks, we have created a powerful approach for extracting meaning from the vast stream of global information.

Looking forward, the next generation of systems will likely become continuous, adaptive, and increasingly autonomous. Intelligent agents will monitor information sources around the clock, discover new content automatically, analyze emerging developments in real time, and alert analysts only when meaningful events occur.

In many ways, the tools and techniques presented in this book represent the foundation for these future systems.

The journey from raw feeds to real intelligence has only just begun.

Appendix

I have broken down the Appendix into four sections:

A) Setting Up a Python Environment

B) Third-Party Python Libraries

C) Python Scripts Developed for the Book

D) Key Concepts

Appendix A: Setting Up a Python Environment

Before working through the scripts and examples presented in this book, it is important to establish a working Python environment on your system. Python is widely used across scientific computing, cybersecurity, data analysis, and artificial intelligence research because it is both powerful and approachable. Fortunately, installing Python and preparing a development environment requires only a few simple steps.

The examples in this book were developed and tested using **Python 3.10**, which remains a widely supported and stable version of Python. In most cases, the scripts should also run correctly on newer Python 3 releases. If you already have Python installed on your system, you may simply verify that your version is compatible and proceed to installing the required libraries.

© Chet Hosmer 2026
C. Hosmer, *Extracting Intelligence from RSS News Feeds Using Python and AI*,
https://doi.org/10.1007/979-8-8688-2773-0

This section will guide you through

- Installing Python

- Verifying your Python installation

- Verifying and using the pip package manager

- Installing the libraries used in this book

- Setting up a Python Integrated Development Environment (IDE)

Once these steps are complete, you will have everything necessary to run, modify, and extend the scripts provided throughout this book.

Installing Python

Python can be installed on Windows, macOS, and Linux systems. The safest and most reliable approach is to download Python directly from the official Python website:

```
https://www.python.org/downloads
```

From this page, you can download the most recent Python installer for your operating system.

Windows Installation

1. Download the Windows installer from the Python website.

2. Run the installer.

3. **Important:** During installation, ensure the option **"Add Python to PATH"** is selected.

4. Complete the installation process.

Adding Python to the system PATH allows you to run Python from the command line, which will be useful when installing libraries and executing scripts.

Linux Installation

Many Linux distributions already include Python. However, it may not be the latest version. If needed, Python can typically be installed using the system package manager.

For example:

Ubuntu/Debian:

```
sudo apt update
sudo apt install python3 python3-pip
```

Verifying Your Python Installation

After installation, open a **terminal or command prompt** and verify that Python is available.

Try one of the following commands:

```
python --version
```

or

```
python3 -version
```

If Python was installed successfully, the system should display the installed version, such as

```
Python 3.10.x
```

or

```
Python 3.14.x
```

If the command is not recognized, Python may not have been added to the system PATH during installation.

Verifying pip

Python includes a package manager called **pip**. This tool allows you to install additional libraries that extend Python's capabilities.

To verify that pip is installed, run

```
pip --version
```

or

```
pip3 --version
```

A more reliable method is

```
python -m pip --version
```

This ensures that the pip command is associated with the same Python installation you will use to run your scripts.

Installing Python Libraries with pip

One of Python's greatest strengths is its extensive ecosystem of third-party libraries. Many of the capabilities used in this book rely on libraries that can be installed quickly using pip.

For example, to install the **feedparser** library used to process RSS feeds:

```
python -m pip install feedparser
```

To install the **OpenAI Python library** used for AI-assisted analysis:

```
python -m pip install --upgrade openai
```

Once installed, you can verify the libraries by starting Python and importing them.

Launch Python:

```
python
```

or

```
python3
```

Then test the imports:

```
import feedparser
import openai
```

If no error messages appear, the libraries were installed successfully.

Using a Python Integrated Development Environment

Although Python scripts can be written in any text editor, a dedicated **Integrated Development Environment (IDE)** can significantly improve the development experience. An IDE provides features such as

- Syntax Highlighting
- Code completion
- Integrated debugging
- Project organization
- Breakpoints and variable inspection

These tools make it easier to understand how scripts behave and to diagnose problems when modifying code.

For readers working through the examples in this book, I strongly recommend using **Wing IDE from Wingware**.

Wing IDE is designed specifically for Python developers and provides an excellent debugging environment that allows you to step through code execution line by line. This is particularly valuable when learning how scripts work internally or when experimenting with modifications.

Wingware provides several versions of their IDE, including

- **Wing Personal**: A **free version** suitable for students and individual developers

- **Wing 101**: A simplified IDE designed for beginners

- **Wing Pro**: A full professional development environment

Wing IDE can be downloaded from
`https://wingware.com`

Using an IDE such as Wing can dramatically accelerate your learning process and make it easier to adapt the scripts in this book to your own research or projects.

Additional Resources for Learning Python

Readers new to Python may find the following resources helpful.

The Official Python Documentation

`https://docs.python.org`

The official documentation contains tutorials, reference material, and explanations of the Python standard library.

Python Packaging User Guide

`https://packaging.python.org`

This guide explains how to install and manage Python libraries, including best practices for using pip and virtual environments.

Wing IDE Documentation

`https://wingware.com/doc`

Wingware provides tutorials and documentation explaining how to use their IDE effectively, including debugging and project management.

Final Thoughts

Setting up a Python environment is the first step toward exploring the capabilities demonstrated throughout this book. Once Python, pip, and the required libraries are installed, you will be able to run the scripts, experiment with modifications, and develop new tools of your own.

Python's simplicity, combined with the power of modern AI tools, makes it an exceptional platform for building intelligent systems capable of processing and analyzing large volumes of information. The examples that follow in this book are intended not only to demonstrate specific techniques, but also to encourage experimentation and innovation as you continue your journey with Python.

Appendix B: Third-Party Python Libraries

Throughout this book, I have intentionally limited the number of third-party Python libraries used and selected those that can be applied consistently across multiple scripts. This careful selection helps simplify the process of building a Python environment capable of supporting all the examples presented.

Unless otherwise noted, all scripts in this book were developed and tested using Python 3.

feedparser: pip install feedparser

A Python library used to parse RSS and Atom feeds. It converts feed data into structured Python objects, making it easy to extract article titles, authors, publication, dates, and summaries.

OpenAI: pip install OpenAI

The official Python library for interacting with OpenAI models. It enables Python scripts to send prompts, receive structured responses, and integrate AI-driven analysis directly into data processing workflows.

Used throughout the book for translation, entity extraction, sentiment analysis, and agentic decision processing. To use this library, you **must obtain an API Key from OpenAI and** insert this into the Python scripts that require it. You will see the placeholder in the Python scripts that looks like this.

```
client = OpenAI(api_key="Your Key Goes Here")
```

newspaper3k: pip install newspaper3k

newspaper3k is designed for extracting and parsing news articles from web pages. It automatically identifies and retrieves key elements such as the article title, author, publication date, and main text content, making it useful for converting RSS article links into structured data for further analysis.

On some platforms newspaper3k does not automatically install and important helper library lxml_html_clean. Thus, you may need to install this manually.

lxml_html_clean: pip install lxml_html_clean

prettytable: pip install prettytable

prettytable is used to create clean, well-formatted tables in terminal output. It allows developers to organize and display structured data such as analysis results or extracted RSS information in an easy-to-read tabular format.

textwrap: pip install textwrap

textwrap is used to format and wrap text to a specified width. It is useful for improving the readability of console output by neatly breaking long strings into multiple aligned lines.

ast: pip install ast

ast provides tools for interacting with Python's Abstract Syntax Tree (AST). In this book it is used to safely interpret structured text such as lists returned from AI responses by converting string representations of Python objects into usable Python data structures.

ftfy: pip install ftfy

The ftfy Python library stands for "fixes text for you." It is designed to repair Unicode text that has been incorrectly encoded or decoded, a very common problem when processing data from web pages, RSS feeds, social media, or scraped content. This can happen when text passes through multiple systems that interpret character encodings incorrectly (UTF-8, Latin-1, Windows-1252, etc.).

Appendix C: Python Scripts Developed for the Book

All scripts referenced in this book are available in the Apress GitHub repository associated with this title. The script naming convention reflects the chapter in which each script is introduced.

For example, Script-Chapter-2-1 refers to the first script presented in Chapter 2.

Script-Chapter-2-1:

feedparser sample script—Acquires the last five article titles appearing in the selected RSS Feed.

Script-Chapter-3-1:

feedparser sample script—Will acquire an article from a known RSS Feed and process that article using to obtain basic information regarding the first article in the feed.

Script-Chapter-3-2:

feedparser sample script with OpenAI sample script. The script will acquire an article from a known foreign RSS Feed and process that article using feedparser augmented with OpenAI to translate the title into English.

Script-Chapter-3-2-1:

feedparser sample script with OpenAI sample script—The script will acquire an article from a known foreign RSS Feed and process that article using feedparser augmented with OpenAI to translate the title into English. In addition, the script will display the results in a prettytable.

Script-Chapter-4-1:

Example script that extracts and normalizes RSS Feed Articles
The script will acquire an article from a URL link provided by the RSS Feed.

Script-Chapter-4-2:

Sample script to acquire, extract, and normalize a foreign RSS Feed article from a URL link provided by the RSS Feed—The script will then utilize OpenAI to perform linguistic analysis of the native language.

Script-Chapter-4-3:

Sample script to extract author details from an RSS Feed—The script will acquire an article from a URL link provided by the RSS Feed and explore the Author Details.

Script-Chapter-5-1:

Sample script to extract NER (Name Entity Relationship) from RSS Feeds The script will acquire an article from a URL link provided by the RSS Feed and extract and report NER details.

Script-Chapter-5-2:

Sample script extract NER (Name Entity Relationship from RSS Feeds).

The script will acquire an article from a URL link provided by the RSS Feed and extract and report NER details. In addition, the script will perform deep analysis of each acquired NER.

Script-Chapter-6-1:

Sample script to perform sentiment analysis of extracted RSS Feed articles.

Script-Chapter-6-2:

Sample script to perform threat analysis of extracted RSS Feed articles.

Script-Chapter-7-1:

Sample script to perform Agentic AI Analysis using an Objective statement examining articles for evidence that suggest emerging cyber threats from multiple RSS Feed Articles.

Script-Chapter-7-2:

Sample script to perform Agentic AI Analysis using an Objective statement examining articles for evidence that suggests threats to industrial control or critical infrastructures that could cause impacts from multiple RSS Feed Articles.

Script-Chapter-8-1-SpaceResearch:

Sample script to perform Agentic AI Analysis using an objective statement to Analyze RSS feeds articles pertaining to interstellar objects, candidate interstellar objects, comets, asteroids, near-Earth objects, and unusual small-body discoveries in the solar system.

Script-Chapter-8-Climate-Change:

Sample script to perform Agentic AI Analysis using an Objective statement to Analyze RSS feed articles for relevance to the global climate change discussion, with particular attention to scientific findings, environmental observations, policy developments, and societal debate regarding climate change.

Appendix D: Key Concepts

Agentic AI: An AI-driven approach in which a system autonomously evaluates information and makes decisions or takes actions based on a defined objective rather than following a fixed sequence of prompts.

Named Entity Recognition (NER): A natural language processing technique that identifies and extracts specific entities—such as people, organizations, locations, and technologies—from unstructured text.

Sentiment Analysis: A method of analyzing text to determine the emotional tone or attitude expressed in the content, typically classifying it as positive, negative, or neutral.

Threat Analysis: The process of evaluating information to identify potential risks, vulnerabilities, or malicious activities that may impact systems, organizations, or individuals.

Entity Enrichment: The process of augmenting extracted entities with additional contextual information from external sources to provide deeper understanding and analytical value.

RSS Feed: A standardized web format used by websites to publish frequently updated content—such as news articles or blog posts—in a structured format that can be automatically retrieved and processed by software.

OSINT: The practice of collecting and analyzing publicly available information from sources such as news sites, publications, and online data repositories to produce actionable intelligence.

Index

Layered intelligence pipeline, 56

Linguistic processing, 48

Linguistic signals, 105

Locations, 62, 63, 71, 85

M

Manual translation, 38

Media reporter, 58, 85

Multiple RSS feeds, 118

N

Name, 61

Name Entity Recognition (NER), 57, 85, 124, 160

    architectural flow of script 5-2

        enrichment, 78–80

        extraction, 77

    bias, 85

    digital forensic investigator, 58, 59

    entity categories, 76

    extraction prompt, 70–72

    foreign RSS feed example, 81, 82

    from article to entity network, 81

    from entity extraction to entity enrichment, 74

    identification, 65

    intelligence analyst, 59, 60

    limitations, 85

    media reporter, 58

    pivot, 60

    profiling method, 75

    reading content *vs.* extracting intelligence, 58

    validation, 85

Name Entity Relationship (NER), 158

Names, 63

National Aeronautics and Space Administration (NASA), 137

National Oceanic and Atmospheric Administration (NOAA), 137

Native-language analysis, 56

Native-language linguistic analysis, 47

Native-language signals, 55

Native-language text, 45, 46

Native text, 45

Negative sentiments, 93

NERExtractionPrompt, 65

Neutral sentiments, 93

Newspaper library, 40

newspaper3k, 156

O

Objective statement, 159

OpenAI, 156

    API key, 17–19

    feedparser, 30

    final output, 34–35

    final script, 30–34

    linguistic analysis, Russian, 47

GPSR Compliance
The European Union's (EU) General Product Safety Regulation (GPSR) is a set
of rules that requires consumer products to be safe and our obligations to
ensure this.

If you have any concerns about our products, you can contact us on

ProductSafety@springernature.com

In case Publisher is established outside the EU, the EU authorized
representative is:

Springer Nature Customer Service Center GmbH
Europaplatz 3
69115 Heidelberg, Germany